WHITE HORIZONS

WHITE HORIZONS

by

MYRTLE SIMPSON

with an Appendix by
Dr. Hugh Simpson

"The first great thing is to find yourself and
for that you need solitude and contemplation
—at least sometimes. I tell you, deliverance
will not come from the noisy centres of civilisation. It will come from the lonely places."
NANSEN

LONDON
VICTOR GOLLANCZ LTD
1967

Printed in Great Britain by
The Camelot Press Ltd., London and Southampton

LIST OF ILLUSTRATIONS

5

Eskimo mother mending one of our Hawick sweaters

Robin and Magdalena

Robin welcomes Hugh back from hunting trip with Eskimoes. Hugh has reindeer carcass on his back, wrapped in its skin, and ptarmigan in his hand

Jacob: Hugh's Eskimo hunting-friend

Reindeer tongues out to dry for the winter

Counting the biscuits: Roger on the canoe trip

Isortoq gorge: Roger battling with the current

Bill canoeing in Disko Bay

MAPS

I

My heart sank as I heard the ring of the front door bell. It was friends arriving to drive us to the airport. In a few seconds it would be too late to change my mind and not leave for Greenland.

A year had sped past, of planning, reading, writing and talking about Greenland, and now with a sickening jolt I realised that time had run out. I looked in the mirror in the hall and applied my last lipstick until September. My hands trembled. Only now did I really realise the enormity of what we had taken on.

We were going to attempt to ski across Greenland, from coast to coast. A blanket of ice, miles deep, weighs down this enormous island, or, as is thought, collection of islands, holding it deep in the frozen sea. This Inland Ice of Greenland is said to be one of the natural wonders of the world. Only a narrow fringe of land is left on which life can exist, but even this coastal strip is ripped into shreds by river gorges, fjords, and a line of jagged mountains of naked rock. Fingers of ice, or glaciers, pour down from the ice-cap to link it with the sea two miles below, like the overflow in an upland reservoir. The Inland Ice is kept back, dammed back, by the mountains of the coast.

For most of the year Greenland is held tight in the grip of the frozen northern oceans, joined as one with the North Pole, Alaska, Russia, Northern China. It is part of the vast, secret world of the North. It is a hungry world. The people and animals living there have to devote most of their time and all of their energy to keeping alive. There is no margin for error. A poor hunter dies, and so do his family, be they fox cubs or Eskimo children.

Historically Greenland belongs to Europe, officially it is a part of Denmark, but its rocks, birds and flowers show an

7

allegiance with North America, and its oval-faced people with their Mongolian eyes stem from Central Asia.

Their world may be grim in winter, but in summer it is marvellous. Light creeps back into their sky in early spring, and the narrow fringe of land around the coast begins to breathe again. The plants and mosses start to stir, ready to burst into flower when the snows have gone. As the sun rises in the sky, this tundra land wakes up. It is a rolling land, dotted with lakes, criss-crossed with streams, and covered with low heath. The traveller from Scotland would recognise the scene: it is like the Cairn-gorm plateau, but instead of being at 3,000 feet, it is at sea-level. The traveller accustomed to climbing to 4,000 feet to see his favourite plant would find it here growing in the valley floors. In places exposed to the wind, boulders and bedrock predominate, and the lichens the only plant to survive, but the greater part of the land is boggy and wet. The heat of the sun can thaw out the ground only to a depth of a few feet. Below, the land remains frozen hard and impenetrable. The water from the melting snow cannot drain away, so it collects in any depression, forming another lake or an area of soggy bog. Because of the narrow depth of this usable earth, only plants with shallow roots can grow, but on the other hand, because of this permafrost they grow well. Little rain falls during the growing months, but what does cannot run away, out of reach of the roots, so each plant has its private reservoir lying trapped on the surface of the solid earth, nourishing it, putting a colour in its leaves and a lushness into the flowers quite unexpected in the so-called "Barren Lands" of the North.

The birds know about these glorious northern lands and start to arrive as soon as the sun. They leave us shivering in the damp and misty gloom of Europe and fly up to the Arctic to build a nest in a crack of a sun-kissed boulder, or in a tussock of saxifrage, warm, soft and dry. The sea birds feel this pull to the North the most. Fat black and white little auks, greyish petrels with their off-yellow beaks, and gangs of noisy kitti-wakes arrive in droves. The ducks are not far behind. Matronly

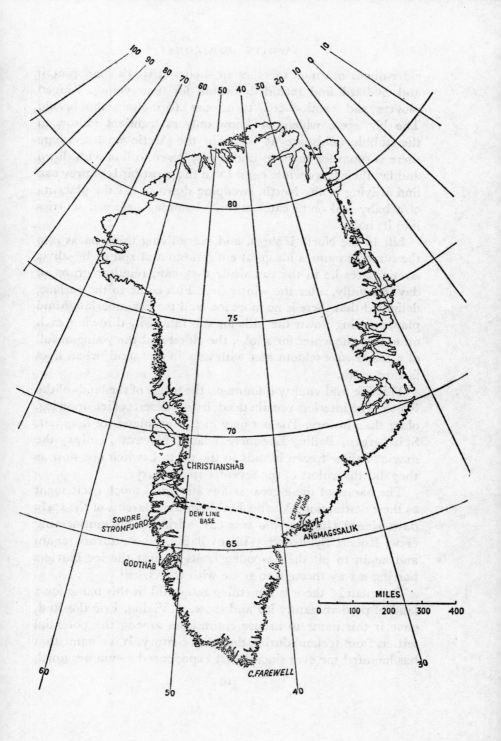

eider-ducks murmur together in sheltered fjords, and pintail and mallard find secluded lochans for their young. Ringed plovers and exotic-faced turnstones trip along the beach. The big geese which we know only as transient visitors in the stubble fields are at home in the Arctic wastes, where there is room for them to find a cosy place to line with down and lay their large white eggs. Even the great birds of prey can find a living in the North, swooping down to eat the placenta of a baby seal or to catch a furry lemming before it scurries into its hole.

Life in the North is short, and every living thing packs into the summer months his great enthusiasm and zest to be alive. Arctic hares lie in the sun while they can, reindeer graze all day, blissfully, after the winter hell. Fish come to the surface, delighted that there is no more ice, and the Eskimoes laugh and play, running down the hills for the fun of it, throwing each other into the water for a joke, the oldest and the youngest full of a *joie de vivre* seldom met with now in our staid urban lives farther south.

This life and vitality is found on the fringe of the lands of the North. The interiors remain dead, frozen deserts of ice upon ice, older than history. The sea may melt, but inland ice does not. Spitzbergen, Baffin, Ellesmere Island, Novaya Zemlya; the magic of these frozen islands to the north bewitch one now as they did the sailors of the seventeenth century.

The names of these great sailors stir up as much excitement as their destination: Martin Frobisher and Barents of the early days, Henry Hudson who was cast adrift by his mutineering crew, Robert Bylot and William Baffin, who returned again and again to pit their wooden boats against the ice barriers barring a way through to trade with the Orient.

Greenland—there is something mournful in this name for a land of predominantly ice and snow. A Viking, Eric the Red, gave it this name to arouse enthusiasm among the potential settlers from Iceland during the tenth century. It is a name that has haunted me ever since I first experienced a summer north of the Arctic Circle. From that time I longed to set foot on its ice, to meet the people who have a way of life adapted to this environment. I come really alive in the North, in the crystal clear air and transparent blue sky, with twenty-four hours of sun shining on gleaming snow. I love the adventure of a world where one isn't cosseted by electric blankets and lulled by washing machines, where there is no National Assistance and there are no people who need it. Not for ever—I enjoy the sophistication of civilisation too, books, friends, luxury, but I like to know that I can do without, for a while.

The Chinese say that a man's life begins with his ancestors and I think that they may be right. Although there is no one in my family who has devoted so much time and energy as I have to putting himself in adverse positions from choice, there are many who have spent their lives in Indian outposts and on the Siberian Steppes, on Burmese railways and in Tibetan huts. They did it to foster the British Empire and they were lucky to find that excuse. People never called them "escapist" as they do me. I bristle at this term. I do not run away from responsibilities and commitments, but perhaps from tin gods, like the television and artificial worries about what the neighbours think. I do not retreat, but advance into a world where to survive one must come to terms with the natural elements. This offers striking contrasts to the artificial values of life at home: of keeping up with the Joneses, of suburban gossip, of getting the better of one's fellows. I look at the boredom of so many wives, preoccupied with empty gossip and tea-cup storms, and living out their unfulfilled ambitions in their children. I love my children too, but I will not saddle them with my own aspirations. I do not feel superior to the average suburban mother but I like to think that my values are not false. I need, though, constantly to refresh my faith in self-reliance, and keep my perspectives true by leaving the town at the weekends and heading for the hills.

This is why my enthusiasm matched my husband's when his line of medical research led us to consider a ski traverse of the vast expanse of ice, Greenland's Inland Ice, a crossing from east coast to west.

Hugh is a pathologist, and intensely interested in stress. Why do mental worries give one man an ulcer and another not? What actually killed Scott on his way back from the Pole? Stress, and the understanding of its effects on man, is one of the outstanding problems of medicine today. Some account of this scientific side of the expedition is given in an Appendix by my husband, at the end of the book.

II

THE NORWEGIAN EXPLORER Nansen crossed the Greenland ice-cap in 1888. Until then, people were prepared to believe that green pastures and a magic world of mermaid-like maidens lay in the middle. Now the world knew that there was nothing but ice.

Nansen's story begins when he was aboard a sealer in the summer of 1882. His ship was trapped in the ice off the east coast of Greenland, and drifted relentlessly nearer, day by day, to the rocky coast. The crew was terrified but he was entranced. Behind the fields of floating ice lay peaks and glaciers glittering in the sunlight; and at evening and through the night, when the sun sank lowest and set the heavens in a blaze behind them, the wild beauty of the scene was raised to its highest. As he says himself, his fancy was drawn irresistibly to the charms and mysteries of this unknown world.

His vague plans for a crossing of Greenland flashed into focus when he heard that the great Swede Nordenskiold had ventured on to the fringe of the Inland Ice on ski and had covered extraordinarily long distances in an astonishingly short time. The nomadic Lapps of northern Scandinavia had followed their reindeer on ski for generations, but few others in Europe knew anything about this peculiar idea of strapping planks of wood to one's feet and shoving off with a pole. Nansen was to show them just what could be done.

He had six companions in his party, including two Lapps, whom he took because he thought that their power of adaption to all sorts of circumstances, and the sense of locality which they must have to survive their way of life in the north of Norway, would add strength to the expedition. Actually, this proved not to be true. They lacked the intellectual ability to understand the need to keep going on. They did not see the point of crossing the ice-cap. It was only Nansen's strength of mind that got them over safely to the West Coast—though Nansen's other companions were tremendous, and as enthusiastic as himself.

Their hazards started when they piled their luggage into little open rowing-boats, and pushed off from the side of the sealer *Jason*, land in sight, but a belt of ice between. They rowed through the floes, pushing them out of the way with a crow-bar. Nansen had absolute faith in his luck. He was well aware of the dangers, but convinced he could get the better of them. The ice jammed and crashed about them, and their boats were carried irresistibly in the wrong direction by a current that was apt to turn into a mill race, hurling the ice floes together, piling them up, threatening to bash a boat to smithereens. They camped on blocks of ice, a man on watch to keep an eye on the surf that could swamp them in a second, and several times their camp site split in two and sailed off in opposite directions. In times of stress, the Lapps went to sleep, and Nansen and the rest laughed. They hauled their boats over the floes that rolled beneath then, and rowed like mad in the stretches of open water, but they could not beat the sea. It drew them back, back away from the land, towards the breakers that could crush them and suck the wreckage into the depths of the polar sea.

They drifted to and fro from July 17th to the 29th when, miraculously, the ice opened and smooth water stretched in front of them, right to the rocky shore of the land. The first thing they did on reaching it was to make cocoa. They had been able to light their stove and cook only three times during the last twelve days. (Their cooker was a revolutionary machine, heated by spirit, but it never quite reached the boil!)

Now the party had to make their way back up the coast, recovering the distance that they had lost in the Big Drift. The Eskimoes they met flabbergasted the Lapps, who were overcome with embarrassment at the lack of modesty of the Greenland women. These two races live rather similar lives, in skin tents, following their food, but their customs and beliefs vary enormously. Nansen had the great knack of a good traveller, to be at home in anyone's company, and was completely at ease in these shaggy peoples' skin tents, eating raw seal and with blubber floating in his drink.

At last they left their boats behind, and on August 15th started to ascend the Inland Ice. They had five sledges to carry the food and camping equipment, which made a load of about two hundredweight each. The equipment included only two communal sleeping-bags, which buckled down over the row of their heads, and were made of reindeer skin, with oilcloth on the outside. This oilcloth they used to cook the supper after a few days out on the Inland Ice; they tore it into strips and lit it on the steel shovel, then sat back to enjoy the comfort of a visible fire. "But," says Nansen, "all the joys of this life are fleeting," and in a few moments their tent was full of smoke. Though they tried to bury their heads in the sleeping bags, the soot on their faces remained with them all the way across.

Nansen had a camera that took "instantaneous photographs", and a massive theodolite that weighed seven pounds, on a stand that weighed as much. With such loads to pull it is tremendous that the Norwegians crossed the ice-cap in forty-two days. They then made a boat from pieces of the sledges, and willow scrub, and launched it into the fjord on the West Coast. They rowed this home-made tub down the sheltered fjord and out into the open sea. They travelled south, rounded a point, and reached habitation. The first European words spoken to Nansen after this fantastic journey were, "Do you speak English?" A laboured conversation ensued, until Nansen realised that he was talking to a Dane.

Since the turn of the century, various other parties have crossed the Greenland ice-cap. None of these have relied on merely their own human resources, but have always supported their party by using teams of dogs, "weasels", "sno-cats", aeroplanes and even a balloon. Yet it has always been in the British tradition to man-haul a sledge, and the technique had been vastly improved in the mid-eighteen-hundreds by McClintock, who spent ten years in the North, discovering hundreds of miles of new coastline, and settled the argument of the only feasible route of a North-West Passage. It was McClintock's success in man-hauling that led Scott to decide not to take dogs to the South Pole. Scott himself had no previous knowledge of the Polar regions when he set out in the *Discovery* in 1901, but he soon lost his heart to the empty, silent wilderness of snow. That is why he went back on the little *Terra Nova* in 1910, determined to reach the Pole. It was when the ship put into Melbourne to refuel that Scott received the telegram "Am going South—Amundsen". This Norwegian was already a great explorer, and there was no reason at all why he should look upon the South Pole as British property. As the world knows, he got there first, and perhaps it was because of his dogs. They tore over the surface, eating up the miles, while Scott and his party slogged on and slogged on, till the time came when they were too far spent to go any farther.

We wanted, on our journey across Greenland, like Nansen and Scott, to go it alone: to pit ourselves against the difficulties of storm, distance and isolation in an environment hostile to man.

But the difficulties and setbacks that an expedition encounters before leaving home are often far greater than any met with in the field. So it was with us. The Danish Government refused to sanction our journey.

The Danes own Greenland. One-tenth of Danish income tax goes to support the Eskimoes who live in Greenland. The Danes are very conscious of their responsibility and provide homes, boats, doctors and dentists. It is not their fault that the Eskimoes prefer to eat raw reindeer meat in their tents far inland on the hunt, rather than work diligently at the cod fishing on the coast. The result is that Denmark pours money into Greenland and very little comes out. Now America also has interests in Greenland. Their "Dew Line" circle passes right across it. The Americans believe that by a series of radar stations they will be warned of approaching atomic attack in time to organise a reprisal. Their stations also provide the communication system known as the "hot line" between Europe and America. The maintenance and supply of these stations is fantastically difficult and involves the Americans in a vast sum of money, and the use of a significant proportion of their Air Force. This means that if anyone gets into trouble in Greenland, the Americans, having planes, helicopters and men in their large aerodrome at Søndre Strøm Base on the western side, are the people to ask for help. The Danes, like many another nationality, don't like to feel beholden to the Americans, and did not like the thought of American planes getting us out of the difficulties they were sure that our expedition would run into.

We understood this reluctance, having the same feeling ourselves. But we felt that we knew the difficulties and were capable of surmounting them, thus justifying the risks. Our party was to consist of four, Hugh, Roger Tufft, Bill Wallace and myself. Hugh and Roger, the navigator of our party, had three years of Antarctic experience behind them and four thousand miles of travelling by sledge. They knew what stretch of sea-ice was safe and what not, where to expect a crevasse, and how not to die in a blizzard. All four of the party were competent mountaineers—Bill, Hugh and I having climbed the highest mountain in Peru, among many other summits—and could bring years of knowledge of mountain weather and difficulties of rock and ice to bear on any problems to be faced in Greenland. We were all very competent skiers, Bill particularly, being a Scottish champion in 1965. But, more important than this, we had all spent years of weekends trudging the Scottish hills in rain, hail, snow, and even sun, amassing our capacities of self-reliance and self-maintenance under adverse conditions. This is what counts when things go wrong.

We had intended to toe the official line, and therefore wrote the appropriate letter to the Greenland Minister in Copenhagen, setting out our plans and asking for permission to visit Greenland. We thought this a mere formality. But the Danish Government took three months to answer our

letter, making correspondence somewhat difficult. Time was
running out. There was only one thing to do. Hugh filled his
pockets with valuable expedition funds and flew to Copenhagen. But he could not persuade the Danish officials to give
him their blessing. We offered to organise a support party able
to fly out to our rescue in case of need. We offered to lay down
insurance money to pay for any plane involved in a search. We
were prepared to offer anything, except give up our plans. No
good: they would not listen. But did we need Danish official
support and permission? More letters were written, to the
Foreign Office and British Embassy. Vital days ticked by as we
waited for replies, but the information was worth waiting for:
by a treaty in the 'thirties a person holding a British passport
was entitled to travel in Greenland. The Danish Government
might not help us, but neither could they legally prevent us.
They would create difficulties for us, but we were prepared to
rely on the goodwill of the people on the spot, and so we con-
tinued with our plans.

Hugh's and my greatest problem was what to do with our
three children: Robin five, Bruce four and Rona nearly three.
As a tiny baby of four months Robin had come with us to the
Arctic island of Spitzbergen, only seven hundred miles short of
the North Pole, where we had gone for Hugh to carry out a
medical research project. I had carried him on my back in a
reindeer-skin cradle, a *komse*, as used by the Lapps, from whom
we had bought it for a bottle of the best liqueur whisky. Robin
had thrived in the clear Arctic air, sucked the gravy from
dehydrated meat stew and cut his teeth on strips of rawhide
used to lash the sledge. As the months of our expedition went
by he had crawled out of his cradle and over the soft tussocks
of alpine flowers carpeting the tundra. There were no germs
for him to catch—no other children to give him measles or
adults to give him 'flu—and most important of all, he was with
both his parents. And Bruce, and then Rona, had of course
come with us in the two following years on trips to Iceland.

Then came the Dutch Guiana jungle. Hugh had returned

from Spitzbergen with theories about what it is in the human body that controls the output of hormones. This output follows a pattern or rhythm each day, and he wanted to find out, next if people living regular lives had super-rhythms. Isolated, primitive people living on the Equator, where there is no seasonal or daylight variation, would fit this category. So we set off for Surinam, or Dutch Guiana as it is more commonly known. Our idea was to canoe up one of the main rivers into the vast secret interior of equatorial jungle, and make friends there with the Amerindians who still live prehistoric lives, happy when well away from missionaries and prospectors.

People had told me that while it was fair enough to take children to the Frozen North, the idea was impossible in a snake-infested, steaming jungle. I thought hard about this and weighed up the dangers, but decided that the importance of keeping the family together was greater than the risks. The two little boys had the greatest fun on the cargo boat across the Atlantic. With all the crew to look after them it didn't matter if I was sick! When we reached South America, we solved the problem of the heat by taking off all their clothes, and I soon found out that snakes do not lurk behind every tree. As we travelled in a canoe as a family unit, the Amerindians understood that we were peaceful, like themselves. There was nothing menacing about us, or we would not have brought the children. The boys broke down all remaining barriers and we were soon just another family in a village of sixteen straw huts. The Indian women loved my fair curly-haired children and I loved their ink-black, straight-haired chubby counterparts, who could handle a bow and arrow at the age of three, and who soon taught Robin and Bruce how to play in the river, and what bits of meat are the sweetest when eating a monkey's hand.

We came home with Hugh's test-tubes filled, and the conviction stressed in our minds that children flourish on family life, be it North or South, provided one adopts the way of life of the local people who are part of their environment. The fatal mistake is to be semi-civilised.

At home, we spend the weekends on the Scottish hills. From an early age, the children didn't have to be told not to touch the primus, or the side of the tent, and gurgled excitedly when they saw a sleeping-bag and snuggled contentedly down inside. This was our way of life and they loved it. Hugh and I just didn't believe in leaving the children behind. This meant that we had to take to hill walking rather than difficult rock-face climbing, and ski-ing when there was a tow and a hut rather than cross country marathons. But we were all together and happy in that.

But we couldn't take the children over the Inland Ice. Weight was too critical. Apart from that, the dangers were too great and very real. The distance was so vast that our party would only be as strong as the weakest member. There would be crevasses, blizzards, biting cold, rock walls to negotiate on and off the ice, hundreds of miles to cover, and a dead weight sledge to pull. Of course the children could not come.

Ideas for a compromise occupied our minds. I lay awake night after night turning them over. Then I had it! They could join us on the western side. They could fly to the American base at Søndre Strømfjord in the S.A.S. plane from Copenhagen. I could end my crossing of Greenland here. I could camp with them while Bill, Roger and Hugh completed the journey to Disco Bay. Difficulties mounted, but now we knew what we wanted to do and were determined to get round the complications. Perhaps I could entice a friend to come out with them, if I could think of an interesting project to do to occupy our time. I approached the Edinburgh Botanical Gardens. Yes, they were very interested. They could make great use of a collection of plants from the area that I intended to visit. Although I had learnt my botany in the field, not in the university classroom, I felt that I could produce a worthwhile collection of pressed grasses and flowers to justify our time and the confidence of the botanists.

Now there was only the question of where the children should spend the six weeks of our crossing. Grandmothers were preoccupied, relatives unavailable, friends busy. But for many years we had known a gamekeeper in Argyll, Ian Duff. His wife Nora might have other priorities than ours, but she was never too busy for a kiss for the children, and her arms were always ready to cuddle them. There were puppies and ferrets around her home, garrons and deer, home-made scones, and thick milk from the cow. The boys could run in the old pine wood and Rona play in the meadow leading down to the loch. They would have plenty of love and fresh air, and I felt happy at the enthusiastic answer to our letter to the little house on the shores of Loch Awe.

Now I could turn my mind, like the others, to the vital question of equipment. We had the great advantage that we had the experience of so many previous expeditions to draw on. What sort of tent would we need? Would our old Antarctic one do, or did we really need to invest £90 in a new one? What was the lightest material compatible with strength? A firm could make the sort of tent we wanted, weighing only forty pounds, but in khaki. Where could we get the same material in bright red? Was it worth the effort of writing to yet another firm? The tent would be pyramidal in shape and double lined, enveloping us in a layer of trapped warm air, with a round sleeve opening to keep out drifting snow. Would bamboo poles stand up to the gales one might expect, or must we go to the expense of aluminium? Everything had to be thought about and discussed.

What would we wear on out feet? Climbing boots would be too heavy, and anyway of no use on the cross-country skis, where the length of stride depends on maximum heel lift. Leather tends to disintegrate on ice-caps, with the constant condensation and drying out. The Norwegians use a very light soft slipper, but this would be too cold and flimsy for us. Lapp reindeer-skin *keskis* like Nansen's would cost the earth. We needed a canvas type of long boot, but where could be buy that? Hugh was wandering home through a depressed area of Glasgow, head down, when he suddenly saw the very thing! A very shady shop was selling off Army surplus equipment.

Hundreds of long white canvas boots with moulded rubber soles filled the window. "9/-, ex-Korean" read the notice attached. The shop-assistant thereupon made the most unexpected sale of his life! There was just one flaw—they were all size nine.

We were all experts at choosing down-hill skis for zooming down the piste, but over-land ones were a different question. They must be long enough to support our weight on the thin ice-cap crust, sufficiently robust not to break on the four-hundred-mile journey, and yet be as light as possible. If we bought Norwegian cross-country skis could they be sent straight to Greenland, avoiding our import tax? Would an edge of hard wood strengthen them enough to last the length of our marathon journey? Should we take a spare tip and pair of ski sticks?—these would weigh two pounds and two pounds was the weight of one man's rations for one day. Weight was critical. Generally speaking, a man can carry fifty to sixty pounds on his back but can pull two hundred on a sledge. But our pile of "necessary" equipment, added to our food, soon amounted to far more than eight hundred pounds. We looked it over and over, scaling down our ideas as to what was "essential". One tube of toothpaste would have to do: that helped the weight problem a lot! And one book each. There could be no question of carrying spare clothes or anything we "might" need or which would "perhaps" come in handy.

Another great headache was that we were really packing for three expeditions. First of all there was our crossing of the Greenland ice-cap. Then there would be my camping with the children; their clothes, food, sleeping bags, fishing-rods, and the presses and blotting paper needed for my collection of flowers. Finally, the men's necessities for the two-hundred-mile canoe trip had to be collected. Two canoes or three? How much of repair kit? Could they rely on catching fish or did they need more rations? Must they take a tent or chance that the fog and rain of coastal Greenland didn't happen?

The question of money kept rearing its ugly head. We had

not enough. There was nothing new in this; polar books are full of such difficulties. Shackleton, Martin Lindsay, Nansen himself, all had the same headache of finance. Expeditions like ours hope for grants from such august bodies as the Geographic Societies and the Mount Everest Foundation. We were unlucky. Hugh then looked for funds to support the scientific side of the expedition, rather than its geographic ambitions. Hugh's professor had an idea. What about the Secretary of State for Scotland? He had funds at his disposal for medical research: they usually went to projects in well-equipped university labs, but it was well worth trying to interest him in our unusual approach to practical medicine. Success! £750! But the expedition would cost about £2,000, and Roger and Bill were as poor as us. Hugh's salary was more than theirs, but we had three children to share it with.

How much is one prepared to prostitute oneself to advertisers? The great mountaineer of the 'thirties, Major Tilman, who has now turned to sail, says he would rather not go on a voyage than have "Oxo" painted on the bows. My attitude is not so strong; I am quite ready to wear someone's make of vest and tell them the result. British firms have always been generous, selling food and equipment to expeditions at half or cost price, and often for free. Considering how little many of these firms have had back for this in the past, I think it is tremendous that they are still prepared to support polar and mountaineering expeditions.

Advertising oneself is a different question. I am quite unable to ring up a newspaper or T.V. company and sell the great deeds that I am about to set out on. I hate saddling myself with the necessity of sending them instalments of our "thrilling expedition". A successful expedition has no dramatic thrills. The papers want death and disaster, we expect life and success. I was faced with the difficulty of impressing the firms that had lent or given us equipment and food that we were competent and bound to succeed, and on the other hand telling editors that we were about to brush with death and to have enough excitement to fill his front page every Sunday for the next three months.

Our overdraft grew bigger and the bank manager more solemn. "Never mind," I announced confidently, "I will lecture all next winter for a vast fee, and all will be well"—forgetting that the organisations that pay a high fee are in London, and that we live in Scotland, where money is considerably thinner on the ground.

In spite of the lack of funds, we could not skimp on our rations. Food was of supreme importance. Starvation is only too well known on expeditions in the polar world of ice and snow. At the end of the American expedition in the 1880s to Ellesmere Island, six out of twenty-five people remained alive. The rest had died of hunger.

This expedition was America's contribution to the first International Geophysical Year: eleven countries took part, and this was before the days of the United Nations. The American expedition was a military venture, with a Lieutenant Greely very much in command. He set off in July 1881, sailed right up the Greenland coast, and then across the Arctic Ocean to Ellesmere, the island nearest to the Pole. Greely's ship, the *Proteus*, left the party of twenty-four in Lady Franklin Bay, a sheltered harbour lurking behind a headland of steep rock. Here the party remained to carry out scientific work and mapping. The boat was to come back for them in one year's time. But the relief ship sank. A sergeant was at this point reduced to the grade of private for disrespectful language. The men were faced with another winter. They all survived, although the doctor was put under arrest for refusing to obey orders to hand over his diary for the official report. No boat came in 1883. It had been crushed in the ice. Greely realised that disaster had struck and that he would have to extricate his men himself. They set out in three little boats and headed south, with fifty days' food aboard and a certain amount of coal. They ran into difficulty after difficulty. Ice repeatedly blocked their way, and the men were freezing in their military clothes. Fog, high winds and waves, and more ice. They were forced to leave the boats and transfer to sledges. At this point the still arrested doctor abandoned the lime juice. Three sledges broke on the first day, but the party staggered on with one. They made only one mile in nine hours, in spite of having twenty-four men to haul the load. They struggled on till October 1st, then realised that there was nothing for it but to winter where they were, with rations for thirty-five days.

They made three huts out of canvas and stones, and filled up the holes with moss. Hunting parties went out, with little result, and the rations were cut again and again. The winter was terrible. The men began to succumb. Frost bite and scurvy crept up on them, one by one, and the first death was on January 18th. The precious rations were broken into, and the culprit was executed on the spot. Greely himself began to fail, and his men to die, one by one. The doctor was threatened with execution too, for helping himself to the dying men's food, and for speaking back to Greely. In May those still left now foraged for sea-weed at low tide. On the 12th the rations came to an end: there was no food left. A raven was shot on the 18th and that was shared out among them. On the 21st some flowers began to bloom in a sheltered place: they ate saxifrage and sea-weed, along with minute shrimps. But the deaths were mounting. There were six left on the night that the hut blew down, pinning the exhausted, spent, dying men to the ground. The very next day, the rescue party arrived. They managed to fan the faint spark of vitality still left in Greely, and in only five more of his stalwart men, on the journey back to America.

Similarly, Scott's party lost strength and became susceptible to cold as a result of inadequacies in their food. But a great deal of scientific work has been put into diet in the intervening years, and more concentrated foodstuffs have been developed, although the same four vitamins feature now as then.

Hugh had noticed in the Antarctic how men reacted to the diet available, what gave them energy, what helped to keep out the cold, and we drew up the rations for our Greenland crossing on the basis of this experience.

Four thousand calories a day Hugh considered necessary, made up largely of fats. I felt quite sick as I stowed away tin after tin of butter, little knowing that I would hanker after twice the amount before the summer was out. Our carbohydrates were sugar and ship's biscuits, a ration of eight a day. The basis of our diet was meat. Dehydrated and compressed, the equivalent of a half pound of meat was packed into a little 2½-oz. packet. Although made from "prime beef", it always tastes like the cheapest mince. I had been on an expedition to the Arctic island of Spitzbergen when I was in the early months of pregnancy and then the meat bar had nearly driven me mad. I hated it, yet was ravenously hungry, and there was nothing else to eat. The sight of the men digging in to overflowing bowls of slushy stew had nauseated me to such an extent that I used to go outside the tent and try to make my one biscuit last till their meal was over. I presumed that my repulsion to the meat bar was entirely due to being pregnant, or hoped so anyway, as we separated the rations in piles to last the four of us for six days. I would never get over Greenland on a biscuit.

Porridge oats, sugar and milk powder, cocoa and tea and dried soup made up the ration, plus a tube of Marmite to flavour the tasteless biscuits "fortified" with vitamins, a bar of chocolate a day each, and a little tin of lemonade crystals for a treat. These were all packed in boxes for the journey to protect them from getting wet; they would be transferred into nylon bags when we reached the snows. Each box contained six days' food and weighed thirty-six pounds. We would take enough to last six weeks. Another six weeks' rations were to be shipped round to the west coast, to be picked up when we arrived at Søndre Strøm, along with the canoes, and spares clothes; also, the equipment that I would need for my flower collection, and anything else for my camp with the children and a friend. What did we need? Toys? Thick jerseys or sun-tan cream? I packed enthusiastically until we realised what the cost of this transhipment was to be. I then took everything out, and we were back to the bare essentials again.

Our small city flat soon overflowed with boxes, bundles of ski sticks, piles of tent material and windproof trousers. Our three children leapt around on top. "Don't touch that," roared Hugh if I approached his study with a duster and moved a clutter of test tubes or samples of dehydrated meat. Maps of Greenland covered the walls and often the floor. But the children still had to be fed and one of them sent off tidily to school. Ordinary life had to go in the midst of the shambles. I often felt I just could not cope. "You must be so strong to undertake such a journey," said admiring neighbours, and I didn't try to tell them just how weak I really felt. It's a strong mind that one needs to get through the difficulties and complications involved with getting away.

Now the pressure of time was stepping up. Our equipment must leave for Iceland on the very next boat. I packed feverishly, while Hugh took everything out again to make another list.

The four members of our party would be living in very close proximity. Supposing we hated each other, I thought, after the first few days? Hugh was quite sure that we would not, and that he had an excellent team. He is a great believer in a "small" expedition for an ambitious project. It is frequently argued that a dangerous expedition is safer when there are more people to deal with any emergencies, but his theory is that more people mean more risk. It requires only one man to become ill or mentally upset for the whole expedition to be ruined. With a small party there is greater unity of thought; it moves faster and is closer to its environment. People are more sensitive to danger if they are not sheltered by an army of others. They know they must be self-reliant and give of their best. And small expeditions are cheaper; nowadays the main expense is in commercial travel, yet grants, and fees for literary projects, are usually the same for a party of four or eight or ten.

Moreover, the whole point of an expedition such as ours is

the effect of a unique experience on oneself; so why dilute it with lots of people? Stevenson alone on his donkey got more out of his solace in the Cevennes than the usual traveller in a bus tour.

I would like to go on an expedition by myself, or perhaps with one other chosen friend, but circumstances usually make this impossible. But the fewer the people one is choosing, the greater the choice. I can be sure of finding two or three people I can bear to share my tent with, and even my toothbrush, but not seven or eight.

Hugh also maintains that for polar travel one needs to be over thirty. The prolonged stress of vast distances calls for a maturity quite different from that needed on a normal mountaineering expedition, where the desperate young climber is at his best. The success of polar travel depends more on mental application than on sheer physical strength. Nansen also made a point of this; he added that his party should be unmarried. He felt, as does Hugh, that between thirty and forty one has the power of both body and mind to meet the trials of such an undertaking. Nansen also believed in his party being friends: there was no question for him of "the leaders" and "the men", as in all British expeditions up to and even after the Second World War. This upper and lower deck idea is hard to understand: surely when one has the common enemy of cold and fear, rock face or mountain storm, one's social background is beside the point?

Hugh's first choice for a companion on many expeditions had been Roger Tufft. Roger is Welsh, but we had forgiven him that long ago. Hugh had first met him in the Antarctic, where they had both been on a two-and-a-half-year contract with the Falkland Islands Dependencies Survey, a Government organisation whose main purpose was to "occupy" that part of the Antarctic continent claimed by the Union Jack. They had made many long, sometimes desperate, sledging journeys together on the Graham Land Peninsula, inland from their base on the edge of the Antarctic continent. Once, with two others, they were on a journey that had lasted for eighty days when they were caught in a tremendous hurricane. The wind tore at them, funnelled up between two ice cap systems. Their camp was flattened. Food and equipment in fifty-pound boxes were lifted into the air and swept away like thistledown. They took refuge in their sleeping-bags, huddled together, fighting for survival. At last the wind abated but everyone was weak and failing fast. Roger was the only one with strength enough to think about looking for their kit, and not least some food. He staggered off with the wind. Eventually they saw him coming back with a bag over his shoulder and a grin of success on his face. The wind was still terrific by normal standards and he had to shout to make the others hear. "Hugh," he roared, "I found only three of your boots. So I chucked one away. Here are the others." Hugh looked at them. One was black, one brown. They were both for the left foot.

I knew that Roger was incredibly kind. He was big, but gentle. He had come with us to Spitzbergen, and I always remembered him sitting with my baby on his knee, cleaning its tiny nails with his marlin-spike. Roger was a sailor at heart so his knife with its spike was always at hand, ready to whittle a rope or knot an end. He came to us straight from an incredible journey of nine months in a little sailing boat across the South Indian Ocean to the Crozet Islands. Their engine had worked for only half an hour on the entire trip, and they had only resorted to it to disentangle themselves from the intricacies of Cape Town harbour.

On the rare occasions that Roger is at home he is a schoolteacher, teaching history. But I do not think of him in the classroom, but wandering in the Lake District, knowing where the wrens' nests are, or the finches', or the buzzards'; or flying my children's kites on the hills above their Grannie's cottage near Loch Ness, and having the patience to undo the knots again and again, while they shrieked with delight. I had canoed with him and climbed with him, played chess in a tiny tent while blizzards raged outside, and had skied with him at home and abroad. He was a man to be with in trouble, and I agreed with Hugh that he was the one for the four-hundred mile journey across the Inland Ice.

Luckily, Roger thought so too. When Hugh approached him, Roger's laconic answer was, "Yes, I've been thinking of that for some time. When can we get away?"

The fourth member of our party must be someone extra strong, to make up for the weak link produced by me. So Hugh had approached Bill Wallace. "Polar travel; four hundred miles of ice! What a journey!" said Bill with enthusiasm. I think he would have said "Yes" at once but he had to consider Maureen, his wife, and his year-old child Fiona, delightful, in spite of a casing of plaster from the waist down—treatment for a malformed hip. Could he leave Maureen for so long? Could he expect her to cope with the difficulties of a child in and out of hospital? He must be at home on the great day when the plaster came off for good, and she took her first step. What about his office? Could he ask for three months' leave, or would he have to give up his job as company secretary to the ship-breaking yard on the Clyde? As a family man, could he justify this step? Hugh thought it worth a letter to the Managing Director, pointing out what an honour it was to British industry for a man on their staff to be invited to join the expedition. To our immense delight the director appreciated this and granted leave and the appointment of another man to cope with Bill's job.

Bill is square, brawn and muscle, with a shock of curly hair, stoic and often silent. The type recognised the world over as a "typical Scot". Like mine, his family home is Edinburgh, and I first knew Bill in my late 'teens, when a bus left Edinburgh on a Saturday afternoon filled with untidy, ex-Army equipment-clad, jovial enthusiasts and headed for the hills. Some were skiers, some rock climbers, some bird watchers, even some fishermen, but we all had the common bond of needing to break away from our humdrum town lives to the adventure of the Scottish hills at the weekends. Hugh travelled in the bus too

(I thought him young and silly at the time!). He and Bill were renowned for their marathon cross-country walks, taking in five or six mountain tops and living on nothing but tins of condensed milk and a very potent type of lemonade crystal that was said to burn up the leather if spilled on one's boots (ex-Army too).

Bill, Hugh and I had formed the "Edinburgh Andean Expedition" in 1958, when our enthusiasm had made up for lack of money. We had travelled to Peru steerage with a boat-load of fascinating Europeans going to make their fortunes in the New World. The only friend Bill hadn't made on the boat was a Madame Parisienne heading for Quito with a herd of Les Girls, where she was to open a night club. Their roving eyes had fallen on Bill, but they were not allowed to linger. In Peru Bill's weight-carrying ability had made up for our lack of porters, and his strength of mind, that gave him the application to cut steps for hours on end, got us all to the summit of five virgin peaks, and two well above 20,000 feet. His enthusiasm and confidence had led us to tackle the highest mountain in Peru, and I shall never forget the thrill of kissing him on the top, at 22,000 feet, the highest woman in the world! Since those days under the clear skies of the southern hemisphere, Bill had blossomed out as a downhill skier. His strength behind a long pair of planks made him a racer of merit, qualifying him even more to come on our expedition. And I knew that his rendering of a Scottish song would help to keep me going many a weary mile as it often had in the past.

But who could accompany the children? I did not have to think far before lifting up the phone and dialling the number of Heather Wheeler. "What?" she said. "Greenland? Oh, all right, yes, I'll come." I had first met her enthusiastic smile and animated face at the Youth Hostel in Glencoe many years ago. She had a flock of boy friends captivated by her personality, in spite of pouring rain and the stark surroundings, and I had joined her group.

III

"WHO WILL LOOK after the children if you both get killed?" asked Hugh's near relations. It was difficult to find an answer. Everyone expects to come back from an expedition, especially me. Getting away for one is far more difficult.

The push mounted. Days tumbled into each other. Half of me longed to be away to the calm and simplicities of camp life, and half of me clung to the yesterdays and the children. We had to let our flat to raise some income. The lawyer came round to make an inventory. He spent all morning writing before I realised he was neatly indenting the luggage going to Greenland. "Oh," he said with relief, when I led him to the cupboard of saucepans. Did he really think that we used billy-cans and plastic mugs in our all-electric town flat? And prospective tenants had to be interviewed: I couldn't bear that woman to sleep in my bed, but could we afford to turn her down because I didn't like her face?

Where in Glasgow do you buy Arctic boots for a three-year-old? How can I get it across to the four- and five-year-old boys that they mustn't go near husky dogs as they might turn round and eat them up? Will plastic net shopping bags over our heads keep off the mosquitoes? And there was Robin's new school uniform to be bought and named before we went, as his first term at Kelvinside Academy would have started by the time we returned. One hundred and one things to be done and no time left.

I couldn't bear to drive the children up to Argyll myself and come home alone. Very reluctantly Hugh agreed. I sent him to the nearby toyshop to buy bows and arrows as a "goodbye" present, while the three of them packed their special treasures in the suitcase. Rona produced yet another "blankin"—her indispensable sucking comforter, of which she needed a mouthful before going to sleep. The boys dragged out a box of discarded, tyreless cars, deciding they wanted them after all.

Suddenly, there was too much time. I didn't know what to do. The children did not realise the extent of eight weeks. The day after the day after tomorrow was as far as Bruce could think. "Daddy's back," they shouted, jostling each other down the stairs, now finding something solid for all the excitement and tension in the air. By the time I was down they were all in the back of our van untying the parcels. I was the only one who cried. "See you in Greenland, Mum," shouted Bruce's high-pitched voice cheerfully, as the car lurched off down the road. But Rona's big eyes followed me up to the empty flat, haunting me as I tidied up the nursery for the last time. Supposing we didn't come back? I had to snap out of my misery to give a lecture at a school on the other side of town, but I did not do it very well.

Roger's great smile welcomed me when I got back, with a cake oozing with Lake District cream. More friends arrived, armed with strawberry tarts. "You'll think of that tart all summer if you don't eat it now," pointed out Roger as I shook my head, unable to swallow a thing, choking on my tears. How right he was!

Then that sickening feeling, as it was really time to go. There must be a good reason why no one had attempted Nansen's journey before, I thought as we sped through the Clyde tunnel. Drinks at the airport. Sudden panic as we realised that Bill hadn't arrived. "Volunteers?" asked Hugh brightly, eyeing our assembled friends. Then we were through "Passports" and waved in that inarticulate way at the farewell party across the stretch of tarmac. At the last minute there was a flurry, and Bill arrived. We were off! The plane heaved itself through the drizzle and gloom of Glasgow into a new world. Sun glittering on a carpet of white comfortable clouds. Cares rolled way. I had already forgotten the trivialities of urban life. A trayful of Scandinavian mouth-watering food was placed in front of me. I sank my teeth into it, suddenly confident. "We'll cross the ice-cap all right," I said to myself, "and soon reach the children on the far side."

At Reykjavik we assembled our luggage—four, five, six boxes. How many did we have? One missing! Hugh consulted his list. "It's the one full of navigation equipment!" The expedition had run into its first trouble. The luggage men gabbled away and shook their heads. Hugh pushed past them and various others who barred his way and jumped back up into the plane. There was a flutter of disapproval around us from the well-behaved Icelandic passengers. Bill and I glanced at each other apprehensively but Roger looked completely unruffled and stalked after Hugh to the plane.

Perhaps we had left it at home. In my mind's eye I could see it, sitting in the hall. Who carried it downstairs? I didn't. Hugh once left our passports on the kitchen table on a ski-ing jaunt to Switzerland. Once he went on a fishing holiday without his rod. Last New Year we went camping for a week without our sleeping bags!

Hugh and Roger reappeared at the door, grinning widely, each with an end of the errant box. Cups of steaming, black-as-black coffee were pushed into our hands. It was Valur, an old friend of our previous visits to Iceland. A true Icelander, he didn't waste words like "How are you?" and "Glad to see you". That's taken for granted. Warm Icelandic hearts make up for lack of speech. He helped us extract the tent, sleeping-bags, and shopping basket needed for breakfast, and we carried these out to the rough ground at the edge of the runway. We had camped here before and knew that nobody would mind. The others went off with Valur but I was too exhausted, and collapsed into my sleeping-bag. I was never so tired again, mentally or physically, during the entire expedition. Once away from the stresses and strains of everyday living, life is easy, simple and calm.

Sixteen hours later, Valur woke me up. "Just time for a swim before lunch." He drove us to the local pool. I staggered stiffly into the ladies' dressing-room, and was somewhat taken aback by the throng of naked, unabashed women. And I'm not Victorian! A smell of sulphur wafted towards me as I headed for the open air. "Too crowded for me," said Valur, leaning against the fence, "I'm not going in." Bill was also leaning against the fence, overcome by sulphur fumes, with a pea-green face, hardly a candidate for an ice-cap expedition. I eyed the three people in the water, then dropped into the practically empty, gloriously warm spring pool. I began to revive slowly and felt more normal and enthusiastic for the new world at our feet. I did full justice to Valur's lunch of fresh cod and butter sauce, and even managed to down some beer.

No regular plane flies from Iceland to Greenland. We had to charter one. We had hoped to share this, and the £500 cost, with a Finnish expedition. They declined when tests showed their motor sledges to be too feeble—so the full bill for the use of a Dakota for a day now fell on the four of us. We sat around the airport taking a proprietary interest as a rather ancient plane was oiled and greased. "O.K." said a young clerk and waved us towards quite a different one just being casually pushed out of a hangar. A very smart air hostess pulled on a spotless pair of white gloves to welcome us aboard. She stared haughtily at my baggy windproof trousers. We fastened our seat belts and looked back at the fleshpots of Reykjavik as the plane juddered down the tarmac. One wave to Valur and we were off!

In a few minutes Iceland had slipped away from below, leaving nothing but the empty navy-blue North Atlantic, with thin clouds dotted here and there. Our air hostess busily pulled on her white gloves again, to give us each a tray of lunch. I regretted Valur's cod! The time slipped slowly by. My eye caught on a line of white ahead. A thrill of excitement ran through me. Ice! Pack-ice. There was something indescribably primaeval about it. Solid water. Flat greeny pancakes jig-sawed together, with here and there the bulk of an iceberg. Like a cross-section of polystyrene. Out of the grey distance, mountains took shape. A jumbled mass of mountains. "Greenland's Icy Mountains". Magnificent white spires and rocky peaks firmly gripped at their feet by never ending shades of frozen, crazy-paved sea. There were so many mountains I could not take them all in. We ran from window to window. Hugh and Roger clutching their cameras, Bill and I just trying to assimilate this new, fantastic world of ice. The air hostess interrupted the view with another meal—smoerbrod—this time ham and cream on bread. "Enjoy it," said Hugh over my shoulder, "it's the most expensive slice of bread you've ever had."

The plane banked and I lost my sense of balance as a mountain rushed up and past the window. We zoomed down. "We can't land here," I shrieked at Hugh, who couldn't hear me above the engine roar. A tiny strip of level ground appeared, a cloud of dust, and we were down, juddering to a halt. The air hostess stretched, then calmly pulled on another set of immaculate white gloves ("Third pair," whispered Roger) and opened the door. A gang of evil-looking men with hatchets leapt in, pushing us aside. A moment's horror before I realised that they were firefighters, and relaxed. I peered out at a clump of bulldozers, U.S. Army lorries and oil drums. A little man with a lurid face and brushed red wool jacket ambled towards us. "Who the devil are you?" he said. "We only heard an hour ago there was a plane coming." We exchanged looks. So much for our worry that the hostile Danish Government might have sent orders for our deportation. However, this was the other extreme—they might have sent some word about our intended journey to the officials on the spot.

Hugh was the first out of the plane, and started to explain to the man about our expedition. Bill and Roger heaved out the luggage and loaded it into the back of a U.S. lorry. I stood and smelled the crystal-clear air. I could feel it, brittle, on my face. I consciously breathed it in, sharp and cold and stimulating. The mess and bustle occupied only a tiny space in the enormous scene around me. I had only to lift my eyes slightly to see over the oil drums to virgin gleaming snow and an empty corn-flower-blue sky. Then I stiffened with excitement when I noticed a white, house-sized blob of ice close beside us. An iceberg! It was swaying slightly in the little area of open navy-blue water at its base, the beginning of the spring thaw. I looked behind—the magic of this Arctic world was shattered. A great "Eye of America" was staring at me. A concrete mass with a radar screen on top. The U.S. have their enormous radar stations at points on an arc curving across North Canada, Alaska, Baffin Island, Greenland and Iceland, where it links up with the N.A.T.O. system whose nerve centre is Fylingdales, Yorkshire. Their aim is to give warning of an atomic missile attack. These Distant Early Warning line stations have the necessary thirty men to maintain them stacked away inside. Their intentions may be peaceful, but nothing could have looked more hostile to me.

The lorry roared into life and we left. The moving cold air felt rough against my face. Two hundred yards and we juddered to a halt. "End of the road," said the red-jacketed Dane. "An hour's walk will take you to the Eskimo village of Kap Dan. No road. Danish policy to preserve the Greenlanders from the U.S. way of life. You can get a boat from there."

We had realised that our plane would land us at Kulusuk, the air strip on an island farther off shore than the main settlement of Angmagssalik, which was also on an island, and still well over ten miles from the coast. But we had not expected to have to start carrying our goods and chattels at this stage of the journey. The two precious sledges were still wrapped up in sacking, sleeping-bags packed in an enormous cardboard box with boots and groundsheets, the food in heavy crates. The tent looked completely unmanageable in its ten-foot-long parcel, wrapped up in a piece of old sack.

The driver waved and backed his lorry loudly down the road and out of sight. The dirt settled. We were on our own! I was suddenly aware that the dry dusty ground was a mass of tiny plants. Purple saxifrages smiled up from tussocks of dark green, pale pink moss campion eyed us from tiny sage-green cushions, glints of yellow turned out to be minute alpine roses, and some of the patches of white I'd thought snow were starry alpines. The boys were already some distance away from me, looking like smugglers with a box on each shoulder, striding over the tundra towards Kap Dan. I picked up the bundle of skis, and staggered a few paces. I couldn't carry it and swapped it for a kitbag full of harnesses and rope. I took out my sleeping-bag from the cardboard box and clutched it under my arm, remembering the old maxim of never parting with your bed. The little path we were following wound up over a col. I didn't try to catch up with the boys. I was so delighted with the world around me. I stepped in their footsteps up a slithery snow slope, then suddenly I could see down to the other side.

What a view! Sugar-like snow peaks were a backcloth to a bay of pure blue, dotted with gleaming white icebergs. A scattering of dark red houses was dotted about the little glen. Out to sea, the ice was solid—a firm grey line, separating us from the rest of the world. The boys were away down below. Dogs were barking and people running out to look at them. I found that I could slither my load behind me here, and I soon reached the first little shack, sunk into the turf with a rack to hold the kayaks off the ground, away from the dogs, I presumed. Three dogs glowered at me, crouching on the ground, with a rumble in their throats. Should I get out of their way or would they get out of mine? I looked about. A crowd of children in a mixed bag of odd European clothes was gathering. Dark, round-faced, pitch-black-straight-haired Eskimoes. They stood and gazed at me with completely dead-pan faces. Black Mongolian, almond-shaped eyes followed me as I hurried on after the boys. "It's miles," I thought to myself with despair as I tried not to slip on the bare bedrock between the scruffy little houses. I could see where the boys were by the crowd. I joined them, where the crystal clear water lapped gently up against the naked rock. A woman with her hair pulled up in a top knot cracked her wizened face into a smile. I remembered from Nansen's book that a beaming face is the Eskimoes greeting to a stranger, as his language has no word of welcome. The old lady wore sealskin boots up to the knee over a pair of ex-U.S. Army jeans, and her teeth were worn down in the front. A cluster of people were standing up in an old rowing-boat with a half horse-power outboard motor ticking over hesitantly at the back. Their language sounded like a collection of Ks intermingled with Gs, but Hugh had gathered that here was a boat going to Angmagssalik with room for only one. No other boat on the island—too much ice. Grabbing my sleeping-bag Hugh jumped in. A stoical old man pushed off with a long oar, and they were away, bumping gently on the flat pans of newly broken ice, twisting and turning out of sight.

I sat down on the rocks, too bemused to think. All this within twenty-four hours of leaving Glasgow! The locals were strangely unmoved by our presence, and we were too preoccupied to notice them much at all. Hugh presumably would return in the morning with a boat large enough to take all our two tons of equipment. Meanwhile we would have to ferry it all over the tundra. Bill and Roger were already on the way back for another load, and I trekked after them, through the rather scruffy settlement, stepping over the dog chains and round the thawing piles of the winter's sewage.

Spring is an unfortunate time to visit a Greenland village. During the winter, the snow veiled any ugliness, and the dogs were kept fit, happy and occupied by hard work. The freezing temperature took care of the hygiene—things didn't smell in the biting cold. In the summer, too, the drying wind ensured that nothing rotted or fermented and the open sea swallowed up the garbage. But in May and early June pools of water lay on the still frozen ground, unable to drain away. Piles of empty tins of dried milk and paraffin were scattered about among fish heads. The dogs were hungry and bored, and so were the people. They could not use their sledges or their kayaks. Their stacks of dried reindeer meat were low and they could not get near the seal. In a few weeks they would leave for their summer camps, pitching their tattered tents at the water's edge up and down the rivers and fjords of the east coast, much to the annoyance of the Danish officials who were trying to organise fish factories and public health programmes as well as education.

The Eskimoes heart seemed to be in the same place as in Nansen's time—a skin tent pitched against the wind.

That night we moved all our belongings a hundred yards off the "road", across a stream, and pitched the tent on a little nest of soft, green willow. Then the red-jacketed man appeared and shouted over "Like a meal? We have all eaten and there is some left." We were hungry and Bill accepted with alacrity. "An odd way to ask someone to dinner," I thought as we walked back along the dusty track. Our friend led us into an empty canteen in the usual Army hut sort of building, and left us to help ourselves to Danish pork and American cream pudding. It looked pre-digested, like most Transatlantic food, and was not cream after all. Raw, fiery schnapps choked me awake and we spent the evening with our mostly silent friend. He was married to a Danish girl. "She lost her heart to Greenland, like me." "Where is she?" I asked, looking round the bare uncomfortable, masculine hut. "She's a doctor in West Greenland. See her often though, once last year she came here for a few hours, and the year before we had a day together." At last we escaped his hospitality. Dry, soft Arctic willow carpeted the floor of the tent. Incredible to think that thirty Americans lived in that concrete monstrosity on the other side of the hill. Americans never seem able to be absorbed by their environment. We breakfasted on Scottish baps and Cheddar cheese, only slightly the worse for the journey. We sauntered towards Kap Dan with smallish loads. Suddenly Roger in front waved frantically to me to hurry up. There, through the ice, a sturdy little boat was battering a way. Hugh was at the bow. "Quick, quick," he roared when in earshot, "off in half an hour, or we'll be hemmed in by ice."

The expedition saw its first action! The boys shouldered marathon loads and I took off the wrappings round the sledges and careered down the shoulder of snow, trying to keep them under control. A wall of ice separated us from the sea, and the boys threw themselves on to the sledges as they approached the brink. I was so frightened of them running away that I let go and stood watching as they thundered down and came to a halt in the narrow run out of soft snow at the water's edge. I was now faced with getting myself down—"Serves me right," I supposed, as I gingerly kicked steps through the icy crust to make myself a ladder.

A tall fair-haired, sophisticated, obviously Danish man of thirty odd was pushing the ice out of the way of a tiny rowing boat. Roger jumped into the water, and in true smuggler's style waded out to the larger boat, a 40-lb. box on each shoulder.

It was good to see Hugh again, but this was no place to chat. I handed the luggage down to the little dinghy. The water was so clear I had the impression that there was nothing between me and the red and russet pebbles on the ocean floor. We would have to make our own way out to the boat. The little dinghy was practically awash.

I funked the cold water and jumped from ice floe to ice floe. They banked and swayed with my weight. One second's hesitation and I'd tip into the icy sea! Always helpful, Roger gave me a hand up the side of the boat. I collapsed on its juddering deck. Hugh introduced us—Carsten Berg-Sørensen —officially Government architect, unofficially a mountaineer dedicated to helping expeditions on their way. The sky was absolutely clear—a calm easy blue, stretching to infinity. The water reflected this colour with an extra tone and texture. Round and about were icebergs, breathtakingly white. The sun sparkled with the vitality of the North. The scenery was so magnificent I could not take it in. It seemed incredible that we were in it, and not Alice peering through the looking-glass. But here was Carsten beckoning us in for coffee. I hadn't had enough of the view. I hadn't assimilated it yet. I wasn't part of it. I hadn't yet thrown off the trivialities of Glasgow suburban life for the immensity of this.

But I was cold. "Come on," said Roger, his open grin disappearing down the hatch. "There will be lots more of it."

Carsten was standing over the kettle, swaying on its gimbal. His sensitive face, well designed like all things Scandinavian, was shaded in a little fair edging of beard. His English was continental. He was a climber, a mountaineer, and I knew at once we were on the same wavelength, and spoke the same language. We didn't have to explain to him why we wanted to cross the Inland Ice. I didn't realise at this time how unique he was! He loved Greenland. He owned a dog team, and when the winter ice crept up the fjords he harnessed them up and spun across the frozen surface, the cold cutting his face and solidifying his breath. His job as Government architect gave him an excuse to visit the outlying settlements dotted on little islands off the coast. His eyes sparkled with enthusiasm as he told us of journeys in the twilight with his school-mistress wife and adopted Eskimo child huddled in the heavy bearskins on his sledge while he urged on his dogs from behind, his shouts ringing in the freezing air. He was thrilled to talk to Hugh and Roger with their experience of the Antarctic and thousands of miles of dog sledging behind them. They started to compare harnessing methods and types of sledge. Bill and I felt out of it and went back on deck.

We were slipping past a shelf of rock and I suddenly realised that the shapeless grey things I took for boulders were tents—Eskimo summer camps. What could they live on? What did they do? I saw something. A man knelt motionless on the top of an iceberg—gazing intently out to sea, watching for seal. Great fingers of rock pierced the horizon to the north. We now rounded a cape, into open water, and sailed across it for four hours, towards the settlement of Kungmiut. Carsten had to inspect a building here—a new fish-drying factory. "Nearly there," he announced, but I could not see any life on the barren-looking shore. We approached a collection of grounded icebergs guarding a little bay. We twisted through and a little cluster of dolls' houses appeared. We headed for a rickety-looking jetty. Splatterings of vivid reds and yellows broke up the blue and white scene. Swarms of children, a smell of fish. Our captain threw a rope but no one thought of catching it. High-pitched, shouting conversations went on with everyone.

Carsten jumped ashore, followed by the boys. I couldn't bridge the gap and waited while our crew tugged on the mooring rope and tried to narrow the stretch of oily water between the boat and the shaky scaffolding of the jetty. At last I could join the others standing in the sun.

The crowd gave way to us, and we walked excitedly up the hard beaten track, towards a conglomeration of little houses, perched each on top of a rock. I could see that, as an architect, Carsten had his problems. How did the houses stand up? I clutched Hugh's arm and pointed breathlessly. A yellow skin was strung out on a wooden frame. It was enormous. A polar bear. The ones in Edinburgh Zoo were half the size. I shuddered when I realised that the huge black leathery square was only one paw! The pelt was thick, deeper than the length of my fingers. "Spent last night on one," said Hugh nonchalantly, "on Carsten's floor." I was suddenly frightened. Who would look after our children if we didn't get home? If we were to meet a polar bear, we would be sitting ducks. I tried to change my line of thought—how did this completely barren land support so many children? "It doesn't," explained Carsten. "They live on Danish subsidies. That's why we're building the fish factory." We had reached a fantastic wooden Christmas tree— thirty feet tall. Dangling from it were fish—thousands of them. Underneath, bored-looking Greenlanders were slowly throwing the dried fish into barrels, to be exported to East Africa. I could see what the Danish Government was up against—Greenlanders obviously did not make the best employees. They needed the stimulation of the chase, the excitement of catching a seal and fending for themselves. This was all right when most of them died in their thirties, and a family consisted of two children. Now most have five, and Danish doctors cured their T.B. and keep them going well into their sixties. Carsten pointed to an old woman with her hair piled on top of her head, screwed back into the traditional top knot. "She remembers when people were so hungry that during the winter they ate the bodies of anyone who had died." It was the only way to keep oneself alive. These Greenlanders in this east coast Angmagssalik district had not been discovered till 1884. Four hundred and sixteen Eskimoes were found by a Danish expedition, living their Stone Age life. This number has swollen to over 2,500 in eighty years.

The Danes found these unknown Eskimoes very preoccupied with the threat of evil spirits that lived in the sea. The people could not explain to the Europeans what these spirits were like, so tried to draw and carve them to put their idea across. They had always decorated their harpoons and spears, with "pin men" type pictures in bone. Now they started to make weird creatures, half men, half seal. Great gaping mouths and hideous "pop eyes". Human heads instead of breasts, extra fangs and eyes. They were "Tupilaks", the evil creatures lurking to get you when you fell out of your kayak, or if you fell foul of the local sorcerer. Unfortunately, the Danes carried them back to Europe as treasures, and now the Eskimoes make them to please the Europeans and the odd American they encounter from the DEW Line base. The Eskimoes can make beautiful things and always have done. What a pity they have now been educated to make horrors. We were offered numerous Tupilaks, which I could not bear to touch, but I saw only one really good soap carving—a beautiful, graceful thing, and the carver was surprised that I liked it. How backward can we get in our civilization?

I wandered up above the fish factory to a little outcrop of rock. Suddenly I became aware of the flowers. Miniature carnation-like pink ones—viscaria; an exquisite cluster of yellow stars—a saxifrage. Tufts of fleecy white petals on a long furry stem, bowing to the breeze. I felt elated and guilty that I had thought the country barren and bleak. I glanced up. The scene was overwhelmingly beautiful—pure white ice and pure blue water and crystal sky. I sat down to bask in the sun. A gang of little boys were clambering up behind me, one outstandingly pale; "Previous expedition, or errant Dane," I mused as they came up. He was the leader, the rest clustered together behind him. He pointed to a big rock, and leapt on top with a bound. The rest followed, but those on top pushed and shoved, shrieking with laughter as a friend plummeted to the ground. A gull flew over—the boys abandoned the game and scampered up the rocks, then froze, and shouted a collection of "squaks". The gull circled, and came back to answer the exact imitation of its call. A shower of stones were hurled at it, and a feather floated gently down through the crystal air. The gull was off, and so were the boys, running and jumping down the rocks, playing at being Eskimoes; and what a place to play—a life to live!

I ran down after the boys and cut through the shacks to reach Hugh. Snarling teeth brought me up with a start. I had blundered into the middle of a pack of chained dogs, and they looked hungry. Hastily I backed and felt rather silly as I detoured right round the houses. They all had dogs, mostly chained, but one never quite knew how long the chain would be. Two balls of fluff came gambolling towards me. A child threw a stone, and they scurried back under a house. Life was too hard to make pets.

I came up to Carsten, testing the strength of a wire-netting enclosure. "Oh, a football pitch!" I exclaimed naïvely. "No, graveyard," he answered, "to keep the dogs out." Graves are shallow here—it's permanently frozen. Sometimes, in fact, the body is laid out on the ground, and stones heaped on top. No coffins in a land that grows no wood. An important member of the community is laid out right outside his house, so the heaps of stones outside were significant. I felt I now had to walk round these too, as well as round the dogs. Everyone else walked in a straight line!

Carsten collected us back on the boat, and rounded up his crew. The engine jolted to life and we were off. The community was soon hidden again behind the icebergs. The wind was freshening. We had to get out before the pack-ice was blown back into the fjord or we would be trapped. He went below and brewed us more coffee, and soon we dropped anchor for the night. Roger suggested that I should have the only bunk, but Hugh pointed out that as I was the smallest, I could fit on the limited floor much more easily than him. I was still so tired with the stress of getting off that I didn't really care.

The Arctic world had its curtains down in the morning. Solid mist enveloped the boat, damp and cold. "Mank", as we would call it on the hills at home. The crew stretched themselves and the engine juddered to life and very slowly we nosed our way forward, the captain obviously frightened of meeting an iceberg face to face. But soon a fantastic line of black peaks began to appear high up in the sky, coming and going behind the mist. Height and distance is relative, and here it seemed to me that these towering rocks were anything from 15,000 to 20,000 feet. Suddenly they were gilded with the sun: a Wizard of Oz sort of world. Slowly the land below the rocks started to appear as the mist crept down. Then it was blown away entirely by a wind that roared straight through my brand new, expensive, nylon and cotton windproof anorak. The rocky mountains shrank from 20,000 to 200 feet.

At last we rounded a point of rock and came into a bay full of ice. Something darted to and fro in front of us: it was a kayak. It rose and fell with our wash, which also made the ice pans clang together. A little man sat flush with the water, wearing his kayak like a crinoline. It has to be the right fit: the women make them to measure. It seemed to jolt me for the first time into the reality that here we really were in Greenland. I had read so much about this world, I knew it well; but it is quite different to be suddenly "in" it. A little white screen lay across the prow of the kayak, and a dead seal bobbed along behind. He was heading for a line of little red houses, curving up the hill in front of us. The red Danish flag flew proudly in the icy wind. We had reached the settlement of Angmagssalik.

It was all very neat and tidy. A lorry appeared, we loaded up our gear, and Carsten drove us to the outskirts of the settlement, pointing out his house on the way. "See you this evening," he said and drove off. Two very fair Danes marched past us and gave us a frosty stare. Obviously social conformity in a community such as this is important and we had flouted it already. No respectable people camped. Soon a delightful collection of Eskimoes gathered around us, grinning widely, and helped chase off the dogs, which were everywhere. I had my first lesson as one ran off with one of the remaining loaves of Scottish bread. Nothing edible could be put down on the ground. "That means boots and leather gloves too," said Roger. He had been up against these Eskimo dogs before: I remembered his story of them eating a Danish nurse. Soon the tent was up and I escaped inside.

Carsten had invited us to dinner. He was feeding his dogs as we walked up to his neat little flat. They were chained but had the luxury of a barrel each. There had been a spare barrel, but a strange dog had arrived, snuggled into the hay and produced four pups. Carsten was one of the very few Danes in Greenland with a dog team. His was of eight—smallish, wide-fronted dogs, well fed and treated as friends. It takes a season of hard work to make eight dogs pull together as a team. There must only be one bitch as two apparently always fight. She runs in the front pair, so keeping the males tearing along behind. Huskies are not intelligent dogs, they would not work so hard if they were, and it's only the British that make pets of them. Hugh tells of camps in the Antarctic where the huge well-fed dogs crowded into the tent and the men shivered outside.

The meal was delicious. "Fresh meat?" I asked. "No, frozen mutton from Denmark, bought one and a half years ago." Danish housewives in Angmagssalik shopped in quantities to last a year. The first boat with this year's supplies was stuck in the ice fifty miles off the coast and was already overdue. Butter had run out in the settlement and sugar was short.

"I suppose you rally together—one wife would run out of this, another of that," I chatted to Carsten's wife. "Oh no," she answered at once, and said no more. I gathered that Danish housewives kept themselves to themselves even more than the proverbial Scot. Why does isolation in a small community so often bring out the worst in women, instead of the best? The men working together and the women at each others throats! Hugh declares he will never go on an expedition with two women as there is bound to be trouble. Although I deny it, I know he is probably right.

Carsten's adopted Eskimo child hid under the table, his impassive face exploding into a smile when I peeked at him round the corner. These east coast Greenlanders are said to be of the "Dorset" type—purer and more Asian than those of the west coast, or of North America and Canada. They consider themselves superior to their cousins on the American continent, and so like to be called "Greenlanders" to differentiate. Carsten's wife told us of some of her problems at the school. If she was cross with a child he would never cry, but would sit with his dead-pan face inscrutable, his arms folded, completely withdrawn. They wore the same clothes winter and summer, coming to school through the snow in a cotton frock and cardigan, or the inevitable thin jeans. The beautiful skin clothes only saw the light of day on Sunday.

"We didn't really expect you," said Carsten as we demolished a rum sponge cake. "One leading Copenhagen newspaper reported that you would take one look at the ice and retire with cold feet." He handed us the month-old paper. The only word I could read was "English". We bristled and all made a mental note to "Jolly well show them". Nansen had more or less the same jeering newspaper reports before his epic trip in 1888. So also did Shackleton and Martin Lindsay. It is interesting that people very rarely send off an expedition with good will and wishes of luck. Is it jealousy on their part, or just cussedness? Carsten, however, was definitely on our side. He thought he could "bend" the itinerary of the official Government boat at his disposal to go near to the spot that Hugh had decided would give us best access to the ice-cap. The "when" would depend on the state of the ice now packing the stretch of water between Angmagssalik and the mainland. We needed an off-shore wind. It might come tonight—it mightn't for weeks.

I felt very far from Hugh as we walked back to our camp.
Frightened of the dogs, I kept close between Hugh and Roger,
but I knew that Hugh and I were no longer husband and wife,
but just two members of an expedition, and that Hugh would
keep it like this all the way. He had switched on his "expedition
wavelength" and dropped a veil between us. Even snuggled
up in our double sleeping-bag I was conscious of a gulf.

There is nothing as eerie as howling dogs. Peering out of the
tent in the morning I looked into a wall of damp, clammy fog,
and wet snow sloshed against the canvas. I knew that the noise
was dogs, but still my spine froze as I listened. Witches and
Macbeth, Dava Moor and death. No wonder the Eskimoes
believed in evil spirits. I could feel that Tupilaks crowded
around, squirming in the mud, clawing at the back of the tent.
I shook Hugh and tried to wake him up, but he only grumbled
and buried his head. I pulled out my pictures of Rona and
Bruce and wished I were at home. I couldn't put my heart
into an expedition when I had left three children behind. Why
hadn't I realised that before? I hadn't got a picture of Robin
and I couldn't remember what he looked like. Were his freckles
on the left or right of his nose?

Hugh spent the day finalising his research technique. He was
going to collect everyone's urine for twenty-four hours, then
retain a small sample in a polythene test tube, having measured
the volume. He had hundreds of these little tubes, all needing
numbering and packing upright in line. Bill helped Roger
organise the sledges and adjust the harnesses that we would wear
to haul the sledge. Roger's months at sea in a schooner had
taught him how to handle ropes and now he practised his art
of whittling ends and joining loops. He always took his boots
off to do this; a view of his knobbly long feet apparently
helped him when doing a "sailor's" job. We filled a kit-bag
with gear we decided we didn't need—in spite of endless
appraisals at home. The farther one goes from civilisation, the
fewer things one considers essential. "I'm not taking these long
johns," said Roger firmly, holding up his pair of new long-

legged pants. "You'll need them," I protested. "No I won't,"
he replied, "I've got my pyjama bottoms, that's quite enough."
I remembered Roger in Spitzbergen, strolling round our base
camp in nothing but a pair of abbreviated pants, while the rest
of us shivered in several layers of clothes. He swam each day in a
fresh water lochan close by the hut, the wind howling down
from the North Pole only seven hundred miles away. There was
nothing aggressively "he-mannish" about this, he just enjoyed
a swim and did not find it cold. One morning he sauntered back
for breakfast, his hair wet and a trickle of blood on his arm.
"What have you done?" I said with worry. "Oh, it was just the
ice. It was thicker than usual, and must have cut me as I
dived through." He brushed it off nonchalantly and shook
himself dry.

"What have you got two pairs of gloves for?" said Hugh
accusingly, eyeing my pile of belongings, "And what is all
that?" putting his foot on my pile of notebooks and the photos
of the children. I relinquished the gloves, but not the photos.

The methodical Bill was attaching our climbing rope to the
roof of a nearby shack. "Climb up it," he said to me, "or you
won't be able to get out of a crevasse." Knowing that the
chances of one of us falling in one of these gaps that criss-cross
a glacier were high, we had brought "Prusik slings". These are
short lengths of line with a loop for one's foot and a metal catch
that allows the climbing rope to run through free until weight
is put on to the loop, and then it locks. This idea is an old one,
and used by mountaineers the world over for crevasse rescue,
or to get up an overhanging rock face. The metal catch is
unnecessary, one can use the appropriate knot, but it makes the
gymnastic effort less if you are a poor weak-armed female like
me. I always find it difficult, the rope swings, the loops are too
long and I can't reach, or are too short and my foot is level
with my ear, and I then have to transfer my weight. If it is a
practice, everyone laughs. I just hoped they would never have
to cry.

A radio station was perched on the hill above our tent. Hugh decided to go up and see if he could be put in contact with the American base at Søndre Strømfjord on the west coast, as he wanted to check up on the position of the DEW line base that we knew was perched on the ice-cap near to our proposed route for the crossing. The Foreign Office in London had given us this information quite openly, so Hugh was really surprised to hear the American drawl over the air, "We have no DEW line stations on the ice-cap. It's secret anyway. You shouldn't know anything about it. I don't." "We didn't want to blow it up," Hugh answered, as sensibly as he could, "but just to know the position as a guide to our navigation across a featureless ice desert of four hundred miles." No good. He could not raise the mighty arm of America.

All our jobs seemed to be finished, so Hugh, Roger and I wandered down to the harbour, leaving Bill to fend off the dogs. "Will the ice go out tomorrow?" I asked one of our crew as he sat on a barrel and had his hair cut by another, and I waved my arm to indicate what I meant. He spoke no English. "Imarar," he answered; I learnt my first Eskimo word, "Perhaps, maybe". Some Greenlandic women were paddling about collecting sea-weed, which they eat in the spring for Vitamin C. A round-faced baby with almond eyes bobbed about on its mother's back as she bent down to haul out a choice length. A piece of seal skin harnessed it into his mother's *amout*, or large anorak hood, keeping it snug and secure. This baby completely disappeared when it saw me looking. The mother beamed when I peeped in to admire him. There were some scruffy little skin tents, much patched with sacking and canvas, pitched at the outlet of a little stream that looked as if it carried the Danish sewage, and we wandered up among them. A kayak was resting on a driftwood shelf, out of the way of the dogs, and a transistor blared forth from inside. "Let's move camp to here," I suggested, but the others were not enthusiastic. What a contrast to the neat houses of the Danish women with their teak and stainless steel! I'd rather have an unwashed smile to a clean frosty face.

I had forgotten a hat and looked for a shop to see what I could buy. We walked past the Greenland Trading Company store and into a little shack. A white enamelled coffee-pot bubbled on a primus and tins of powdered milk jostled for space between packets of contraceptives, coloured beads, gum-boots and the inevitable jeans. Cups of black syrupy coffee were expected to be drunk from chipped white fluted cups before any business took place. Soon the little café-cum-shop was full of round-faced Greenlanders ready to help me choose. There only was one kind of hat, a red wool beret, but the shopkeeper insisted on me trying on every one of his identical stock. A strident record burred round the gramophone on the counter. I wondered how many people would help me try on one of the enormous white cotton brassières hanging up on a peg if I had decided to buy one of those as well.

On the way back to the tent we passed the fire station—two red sledges drawn up outside with enormously long whips poised at the ready—an indication of speed! Now it was my turn to be watch-dog to the tent, so I lay on my sleeping-bag and tried to read.

I found it difficult to become interested in the local scene or make friends here, when my mind was preoccupied with the marathon journey in front of us. My book was *The Chapman Report*—an account of sophisticated American women. What a contrast, I thought, as I looked at my already grimy fingernails and unwashed socks. I brought this book only for reading on the plane, but had then been too excited to open it. The choice of what to take on an expedition is interesting. Some travellers look for long, complex Russian novels to occupy their minds. I have often thought that Dickens would be good, the detailed and involved lives and situations so different from a world between four walls of a tiny tent, but I have never actually convinced myself enough to rely entirely on him. I prefer to use my mind playing chess, and need a lighter book to interest me without much effort on my part. When I am physically exhausted, my brain is too. I do not think deep thoughts on an expedition, but at home, pottering over the kitchen sink.

For this crossing of Greenland, we had rationed ourselves to one book each. Hugh made his choice instantly, a tome on pathology. Since becoming a medical student, seventeen years ago, he has had practically no time to read anything but the vast flood of medical literature necessary to keep abreast with new ideas and research. Bill was just as involved with his profession, his book was on business management; he insisted he had to read it to keep him in tune for an exam scheduled for our return. Roger's choice was Churchill, *My Early Life*. Mine was *The Blue Nile*. I thought the contrast of African deserts and old civilisations would interest me in our world of ice and snow. Roger and I spent the entire expedition warding the other two off our books. Theirs remained unopened.

As well as these four volumes, we had Nansen's *First Crossing of Greenland* and Roger's various "Aids to Navigation". I was rather worried when I saw *Teach Yourself Navigation* in his pack, but he said he brought it only for the log tables in the back.

Soon the others returned and threw themselves down in the tent, idle and dejected. After our push to get off, this waiting about was intolerable. There was a noise outside the tent— Hugh was just about to throw a curse at a dog when a bearded face looked in at the door. "My wife asks you for coffee." We all leapt to accept, and followed the man to the little house at the back of the tent: our nearest neighbours! His wife was very young and delightful, and made excellent cake. She spoke no English, but we nodded to each other enthusiastically and spent the evening looking at their books. It was an effort to leave their upholstered chairs and ready hot water for the tent. At last we prised ourselves out. On the way back Roger nonchalantly announced that he had forgotten to tell us that Cartsen has "fixed the boat for us for tomorrow, on the 9 a.m. tide".

It was a glorious morning. The sun streamed through the tent door. It was Rona's third birthday, I remembered, with a catch in my throat. We stuffed away our belongings and took

down the tent just in time to look as if we had been ready for
hours when Carsten drew up in his lorry. We screeched down
to the harbour, brakes full on, and jumped out on the wharf.
There was great activity aboard the little orange boat, pock-
marked from contact with the ice. Dozens of hands helped us
stow away the gear, and the two sledges were balanced on the
deck. There were two hunters aboard, blasting off bullets into
the crystal sky, testing each other's guns on little pieces of ice
that were bobbing innocently up and down with the tide. Fair,
fair Danes were clustering on the jetty to wave us off and
a gathering of bejeaned Greenlanders jumped up and down,
shouting to our crew excitedly. Every joint in the boat creaked
and shook like a Clyde puffer as the engine put up steam. Water
appeared between us and the jetty. We were off! The little
houses shrank into their surroundings, then we rounded a huge
berg, and were alone. I took a deep breath.

After a while we noticed that there was an argument going
on in the wheelhouse. The captain was shouting into his crack-
ling radio and Carsten's unruffleable face was a shade darker.
He came out and shrugged his shoulders. "Got to go back—a
plane is due at Kulusuk and the passenger needs this boat to
come across to Angmagssalik. A Government official, so the
captain has got to obey."

The farewell party had disbanded. What an anticlimax! No
one helped us to throw our gear ashore again. Perhaps the
Copenhagen paper was right and we wouldn't get on to the ice.
I felt rather a fraud as we wandered back up through the
houses. Our bearded friend saw us and beckoned us in for
lunch. Ten or twelve little tins of gaffelbitters, fish-liver paté
and anchovy to lay on bread. How do the Scandinavians
manage it? I would need twenty tins a day to feed my family at
home and they would still ask for a square meal. I nudged the
boys under the table as they emptied tin after tin. As usual
Hugh failed to get the hint. "What's the matter?" he asked
in a loud voice turning round, "That's me you're kicking!'

"Come fishing?" said the husband, picking up a pole and a

length of twine and several large hooks. We followed him inquisitively as he led us up the glen leading from the settlement. It was delightful. The sun shone on the new green grass, splashed here and there with little clusters of tiny flowers. A circle of rocky mountains converged in front of us. We scrambled up a little gorge and came to a partly frozen lake. Our friend strode on to it, clutching his pole. Quite far out he bashed at the ice till he made a round hole. He lowered his line and stood stock-still, except for his right arm that constantly twitched the tackle. Hugh and Bill followed suit but considerably nearer shore. I lay on the smooth, sun-kissed, ice-worn rock and laughed. They looked so daft.

Soon my eyes were drawn to the top of the cirque above us. Rock walls rose to about 2,500 feet, but an easy angled ridge, well spaced with grassy ledges, offered an obvious route to the top. Roger saw my intention, and we walked round the lake and scrambled up the steep scree slope to a little col which gave us a view to the sea, pale blue, with green pans of ice swaying in the tide. We went on up easy scree slopes, till we reached the snow. I was quite far up it before I realised that it was really steep and getting worse. The surface of soft, kickable snow lying on hard packed ice was getting thinner. We had no axes, crampons or boots. But it was definitely easier to go on up than down. Little avalanches were set off by our feet as I concentrated on getting across to the sky-line ridge. It turned out to be of rotten, loose jumbled rock. I hated it, but Roger was above me, and his moral support seemed to give me a physical belay. I gingerly placed my foot on the rock, transferred my weight on to it without upsetting the pack of cards, and inched the other forward to gain some height. The corner of my eye showed me a drop straight down to the lake on one side, the sea on the other. Then I bumped into Roger. He was sitting on the top gazing transfixed to the west. I turned my head and caught my breath. A great wave of white surged up, filling the horizon, obliterating the sky. The Inland Ice! I felt ecstatic, then horribly afraid. It was enormous, endless. Who were we to pit ourselves against it? How could we possibly cross it? "Come on," said Roger. The sun was round behind us now, the snow slope in shadow. The snow would be frozen hard. Impossible with our canvas shoes, which would never get a bite into the surface. There was another way off—down the far side, that swept in a gentler angle to a hanging valley a thousand feet below. If we went this way it would mean miles of walking round the foot of our mountain to get back, but anything was better than descending that rotten ridge and then the frozen snow. So now we faced the sea, with white icebergs bobbing in the blue moving water, but cut across a few miles out by a line of solid pack, stretching to the horizon. Somewhere out there were the frozen assets of the Angmagssalik housewives' larders in the hold of the ship that had come from Copenhagen, now stuck fast in the ice. There were no birds. It was a dead silent world, and it was late into the night when we staggered into Carsten's house to join the others, just about to demolish another rum sponge cake.

IV

We were really off! Carsten's wife had thrust two loaves of soft new bread into my arms as she waved us off at 5 a.m. The seal hunters were again abroad, shooting off bullets at anything that moved. Two gyr falcons appeared from a cliff, but, thank heavens, they soared away out of reach. The hunters wore boots of sealskin, lined with soft, thick husky dog fur at the feet and tougher, long-haired seal about the calf. "Kamicks," said the owner, when he noticed my admiring looks. "What's that? Cami-knicks?" said Roger, his eyes lighting up.

The sky was a brilliant blue. Not a cloud to be seen. But a keen wind seared right through my anorak, chilling me to the bone. When would I be warm again, I thought. The night's frost had formed new ice in the bay, but our boat had smashed through. We had rounded the island and were now crossing the open water towards the land (see map facing page 76).

Gino Watkins had been here before us. In 1930 he had led an expedition to find out the possibilities of an air route between Europe and America. These were the early days of aeroplanes and the fact that the shortest line between England and Canada lay straight through Greenland was important. The least known part of the proposed route was the East Coast and the Ice Plateau of Greenland, and Watkins and his men were to try to find out something about it. They set out with the intention of establishing a base on the East Coast, and from there making journeys north and south to map the coast, but also to travel inland and leave a party of men midway between east and west, to winter over. They were to take weather observations and try out the flying conditions from a hut that was to be sledged out during the summer months. Watkins was lucky that in 1930, in spite of trade depressions, people were thrilled by planes and the air. Money was raised for his ambitious plan because the eccentrics of the time were all gripped by enthusiasm for this super new thing with wings. In those recent days, too, the public's imagination was not all spent on gazing at the television screen, and the ordinary man was thrilled by the enterprise and vision of a traveller to the North.

Gino, the hero of the 'thirties, was twenty-three, with that urgent love for Arctic regions well established, but his party of thirteen were nearly all new to the North. Watkins did not like his companions to have previous experience. "I prefer that all members of my expeditions should have gained their knowledge with me, since in that case I always knew the exact amount of experience possessed by each member of any sledging party. If anything goes wrong with one of these parties and it fails to turn up at the proper time, I can judge more easily what the leader of the party will do in an emergency." To me this idea is extraordinary. Dare one, in 1966, criticise our parents' blue-eyed boy, even though he did get himself killed at the early age of twenty-five? Surely better for his men to be able to extract themselves from their difficulties than unable to because Gino had not told them how? His name has gone down in history because he was a brilliant "leader of men". I prefer companions that do not have to be led, who will talk over the situation and listen to each other's point of view. Of course, one can have too many captains in a two-man canoe, and flounder on the rock in the middle because each wanted to round it on a different side, but in the Arctic, each man must be responsible for his own life and make his decision for himself. However, it is interesting to find nearly all the names of Watkins' party featuring again and again in the story of Arctic exploration in the years to come.

Their expedition sailed down the Thames on a brilliant sunny day in Shackleton's wooden boat, the *Quest*, which has featured in so many epics of the polar seas. The Eskimoes they met with in Angmagssalik were far less influenced by Western ways than ours thirty years later, and I envy them this precedence of time. Perhaps nowadays less Eskimoes die of

T.B. or drown, but I feel furious with the generation that has destroyed a way of life that was blooming when I was born. The Watkins' party chose a spot for their base on the mainland, in a green valley leading up to a mountain top, with a glacier flowing down in easy stages to stop just short of the sea. They erected their wooden hut and the hangar for the two de Havilland Gypsy Moths, as well as for sacks of coal. They had a motor to give them electric light, two 70-foot wireless masts, and fifty dogs.

To me, the epic of Watkins' expedition was the establishment of their ice-cap station. It was to study the weather and to see if there was a valley, or any depression running across the ice-cap, which would be of significant value to the pilots of the proposed air route, whose little planes of those days were very susceptible to air pressure and wind. After tremendous effort, the dog sledges at last reached a point at 8,600 feet, and the men erected a dome-shaped tent with a living space of ten square feet, smaller than most bathrooms. Here two men spent a month organising the meteorological equipment and trying to build an igloo to increase the floor space of their tiny world. They then returned to their base and Augustin Courtauld took their place. This was December and the plan was that he would stay until March.

Courtauld's first relief party spent three weeks in the vicinity of his ice-cap station but so appalling was the weather that they used the time fighting for their own lives rather than searching for someone else, and returned without finding a trace of him. Gino then went back to look again with another team and this time they were lucky.

Courtauld was completely alone for five months before his friends found him and brought him back to base. To begin with he was busy storing his stores and reading his instruments. But to get to them he had to dig his way through the tunnel from his tent to the outside world. Gradually the drift got the better of his digging and he realised that he was about to be buried alive. He was digging from the inside and so there was nowhere to dump the debris without filling up his living area, so he had to give up. He managed to make an entrance into one of the snow houses for a while and so gain the open air, but again the weather got the better of him, and he retired to the drifted-over tent. The walls sagged from the weight of snow, cutting down his space to seven or eight feet, and he now discovered that most of his paraffin had leaked away.

He knew that his life depended on his ventilator. Without fresh air, he would asphyxiate. He was also well aware that from outside his underground house would be invisible and that the relief party would very likely pass him by. However, he cheerfully resigned himself to waiting until the spring, absolutely confident that Watkins would come then.

Many trappers and prisoners have spent months by themselves, but no one in a situation such as this. He was interested in making the weather recordings which gave him a purpose in life, but when he had to abandon these, he felt that he was completely wasting his time. He had to spend more and more hours in the dark, his home getting colder without the heat of the lamp. He had food, but did not want it, and was satisfied with half a pound a day. Condensed moisture covered the inside of his tent, hanging down in long icicles from the roof. His tobacco ran out so he substituted tea. To start with, the silence of his surroundings affected him so that he could not bear to make a noise, but this changed to the point where he satisfied himself by singing an endless dirge.

The months dragged by, until on May 5th the primus gave its last gasp and died. He was just wondering how to make out without it when he heard a scratching, scraping noise. The relief party had arrived.

Courtauld looked like a biblical fanatic, with long, unkempt, curly hair and a great dangling beard, and his tent a hoary cave. His face was thin and ingrained with grime, but he was well in body and mind and could walk in spite of the endless days in his sleeping-bag.

He soon regained his strength and instead of returning to

England he embarked on a six-hundred-mile journey with Gino and one other in an open boat to explore the fjords south of their base. They lived like Eskimoes, off the land, and nosed the little boat with its outboard motor inshore between ice and coast. They rounded the southern tip of Greenland, and then up the friendly, Irish-like, south-west coast to their destination, with only one gallon of petrol to spare.

The British Arctic Air Route base camp had been at a point just out of our sight, right round a headland sticking out into the sea blocking our view. From there a glacier swept down to the sea-level at an easy gradient. Hugh had read and re-read Watkins' account of their ascent on to the ice-cap from this camp, up an ice-fall they called aptly Bugbear Bank. Hugh had managed to inveigle aerial photos of this area out of the Danish Geodetic survey. He had spent the winter peering at these and the ones of 1930 and knew every inch of the route, every crevasse, every fold in the ice. He knew exactly where he wanted us to go; the route to follow that would get us up on to the Inland Ice.

We changed course, zigzagging between great clumps of floating ice. I thought of the *Titanic* and how cold it could be. There was an ominous line ahead: pack-ice. The captain revved up the engine and charged. Crack, graunch, we made a little headway, rode up atop of it, and then slowly subsided as it broke beneath our weight. We reversed, then charged again, and made a few more feet. The Eskimo in the crow's-nest waved his arms and shouted, and the captain left the wheel to clamber up to join him. He poised on the ladder, gently swaying, gazing intently ahead, looking noble and completely in command. Not so long ago the boats in these waters were under sail, the sailors handling frozen ropes and acres of stiff canvas. How did they manoeuvre their ships? How did people like John Davis ever reach his destination, or Cook and James Weddell of the southern polar seas? Few of our generation would have the incredible strength of mind of the early Arctic travellers, whose journey lasted for up to five years and whose food was salted pork. Hugh stood at the prow looking worried. It was obvious that our boat would never make it round the headland into Suportoq Fjord. Sure enough, the captain came down and shrugged his shoulders at Carsten. He changed direction and tried again. This time we crashed through the ice. It broke up in front of us—great green flat pans riding into each other, revealing boiling, broiling masses of inky black water of infinite depth. We forced a way through and reached a lead, twisting and turning, then bulldozing through the ice again.

This was all very well, but my elation was not matched by Hugh's expression. We were sailing east instead of south. He joined Carsten and the captain in the wheelhouse. The grey walls of the coastal mountains were near but I couldn't judge how near because of the false effect of ice, water and snow distorting the image.

Carsten and Hugh gazed through the captain's binos. "Carsten says the Eskimoes have a sledging route up there, over and down to Isortoq, a little settlement beyond the 1930 base, but none of the crew have done it. Shall we risk it?" What should we do? The decision was vital. The alternative was to return to Angmagssalik and wait for another chance, but wasting valuable time. We were standing out in the freezing wind and I for one felt anything was better than more hours on the boat. Roger and Bill were all for getting off here. Hugh had misgivings. I didn't care.

Suddenly the captain fished in his pocket and handed me a letter. It had come in yesterday's plane. The round hand of the gamekeeper's wife brought a lump in my throat as I tore it open. Tears splattered on to the page. I brushed them away and read that the children were happy, but Rona was frightened of the dogs. Bruce had fought with a girl in the village and Robin had been all the way to Lochgilphead "to see the doctor because of his chest". What did this mean? I read and re-read the letter. Nothing else. A row of kisses were scratched along the bottom and the children's intent faces flashed in front of me as I visualised them patiently writing them out. Oh God, why had I come? Why had I left them? Darling little children! What was the matter with Robin's chest? The gamekeeper's house was teeming with dogs, Rona would never get away from them. Bruce only fought when very provoked. "I'm not coming," I blurted out. But Hugh didn't hear. He was too preoccupied, questioning the crew about the lie of the land, and willing the boat to go a little nearer the shore, at least into the mouth of Johan Pedersen Fjord (off Sermilik). The happy-go-lucky hunter came up to me. He was holding his kamicks. "For you," he said and thrust them into my hand. I threw all my emotion into gratitude, and overwhelmed him with my thanks.

"Come on, get off," shouted Bill, echoing the accents of the Glasgow bus conductresses, and I realised that the engines had stopped. We were to be put down on the sea ice here. Hugh was already walking about round the boat clicking his camera, and Bill was throwing out the luggage to Roger. All the crew helped. I hesitated. I could not believe that the ice could hold our weight. There was the boat floating in water and Roger leaning against its side, his feet on dry ice! It was so outside any experience! Bill felt the same. He saw me looking at him, and jumped over the side. I felt again that agonising impression of fatality that one has when time catches one up. A dreaded exam paper is actually in front of you. The dentist's receptionist calls your name. You stand up in a hall full of people waiting to hear you talk. It's your turn next down the ski-race course. This is your step off the ground on to the rock climb. Reluctantly I relinquished the safety of the boat and followed suit. I landed in slushy snow. It gave beneath my feet. In fact it actually swayed. I know what the man will feel who first steps out on the moon. I don't know why, but I suddenly felt enthusiastic. Nansen got there. Why shouldn't we? Hugh and Roger loaded up the two sledges while Bill and I unravelled the harnesses. The captain then leant over the side and threw down a large codfish, which landed with a thud at my feet. Bill added it to the load on the sledge.

We were ready. "You've forgotten something," said Carsten and handed me an enormous almond cake. "I have never seen an expedition so well organised. I am sure you will succeed." He shook my hand and I felt proud of his faith in our little party. If he believed in us, so would I.

It was better for the crew to watch us go, rather than us stand and watch them. "Come on," I urged. Bill and I were to pull one sledge, and to my surprise it moved quite easily. Bill burst into the Tay Boat Song and I strode along at his side. We covered a few hundred yards and then the sledge started to stick. One of my feet sank, then the other. I floundered up to my knees. Terrified of going right in, I screamed to the others. The two of us heaved at the sledge, moving it. But I felt like giving up; I was sopping wet, we were miles from the shore. Great holes of black water lay about, glimpses into the bowels of hell. But I couldn't get any wetter and started to do a bit better. Bill and I could manage the sledge alone again. I wouldn't panic if I didn't think of the distance, but only of the next few steps. Ours was the leading sledge, and we plodded on straight across the thin places, ignoring the swaying ice moving with the rise and fall of the tide. A little shelf of dry ice came up. "Let's camp," said Bill. I didn't remember ever being so tired. The others came up and queried our choice of site, but Bill and I had had it. Soon we collapsed into the tent. Bill, sodden through, was snoring as soon as his head hit the ground-sheet. Roger helped me haul off my sopping clothes, but I came to life when Hugh had the primus roaring out heat. Our world had a limit now the tent was up, and I bit into Carsten's almond cake with enthusiasm. Hugh attacked the fish and cut it into steaks, while Roger melted fat in the pan. It frizzled and spat, but I was too tired, and after one little bite I gave up and rolled into the sleeping-bag that Hugh and I shared. He and Roger ate most of the fish and talked enthusiastically for hours on end. They were at home on the sea ice and unperturbed. Bill and I were worn out, unused to this strange world of bending, swaying, frozen sea.

Leaving the boat on the East Coast

Myrtle leading off

Rotten sea-ice at the start: Myrtle, Bill and Roger

Sledging on hummock ice: Myrtle and Roger

Approaching a crevasse

Crevasse
crossing

Roger and Bill on a snow bridge

The snow was far from smooth

I was stiff in the morning. We stirred at six, hoping that the night frost would have put a crust on the ice of the fjord. Cod steaks for breakfast. Bill and I were still tired and squabbled over the primus. "Pump it up," said Bill. "No, it doesn't need it," I said. Then I heard myself shouting at Hugh, who was wearing my cagoule instead of his. These were identical, red nylon over-anoraks that came down to our knees. The fewer possessions one has, the more precious they become; and the less privacy, the more important one's own corner of the tent. "My" gloves, although they were eactly the same as the others. The possessiveness of adults when reduced to fundamentals drops to childlike levels. One retains a sort of security by always sleeping at one side of the tent, always using the same spoon, although there is one each.

I have heard my children squabble about who is sitting where round the kitchen table, as if it really mattered, and now I heard us doing the same. Roger, quite unmoved, got on with packing up the tent. It was fantastic how the sledges could accommodate everything at last, even the remaining fish.

What was round the corner? Would we find a glacier sweeping down to the sea? What if we didn't? Hugh and I were together on one sledge and it needed an enormous heave to overcome its inertia. Huge icebergs were frozen in here and we moved between them. Suddenly, I crunched through to icy water. My feet were agony. I was sweating above the waist, dying of cold below. We floundered on, trying to catch up with the others. They stopped for us, sitting disconsolately on their sledge. We soon saw why. We had rounded a point and now had a view to the head of the fjord. No glacier. A solid bank of rocks blocked our way up to the ice-cap. We all gazed at the rock wall hopelessly.

But we could not go back. A wraith of snow zigzagged up diagonally. It might be a route. We moved on, but in a few minutes Hugh and I were both up to our waists in a morass of slush and water. Four on a sledge and we still couldn't gain any ground. The sledge was bogged down completely, its runners buried in wet snow. Without losing heart, Roger and Hugh untied the load, jettisoned half of it, and put on their skis. Bill and I were to push from the back. With four of us now on a light sledge we moved on. Two steps on dry ice, then crash, through to one's thigh. Every time I put my hand on the sledge I came in contact with the floppy, slimy body of the dead fish. I began to hate it. I slipped and my face slapped against it.

On and on. I didn't dare look up to see how far we still had to go. The "few miles" turned out to be twelve, but at last we reached a little waterfall spurting out over some rocks before it was buried in the ice of the sea. We came to a halt. Roger walked about, looking for a good site for the tent. Suddenly he vanished, except for his hands, clutching the edge of the ice. Hugh and Bill charged forward while I fumbled with the rescue rope, supposed to be "at the ready" on the back of the sledge for just such an emergency. They heaved and hauled, grasping his wrists, and landed him, his red hat still on and his smile frozen on his face. Quickly we stamped down the soft snow to make a platform for the tent and pushed him inside with the primus.

Back we had to go, again and again, for the rest of the load. Completely exhausted, I sank down at last and peeled off my sodden socks and boots. I slipped my feet into the kamicks. They were soft, dry and sensually comfortable. Glorious sun sparkled down at us as we cooked the fish outside the tent. There was no wind. Utter silence and peace. Life was good. Then suddenly, the sun was behind a hill and it froze at once. It was marvellous in the tent and Hugh unpacked the little radio, brought for Roger's navigation. Time would be critical to him when he was using his sextant on the plateau. A second out in time meant miles in direction. Bill fixed the aerial on to a ski stick and Hugh twiddled the knobs. Suddenly the tune I was to know so well filled the tent: "Lilliburlero". "This is the British Overseas Programme. Here is the news." I had to force myself to listen. I wasn't interested in the Algerian revolt, and the Prime Minister's difficulties seemed so trivial when sitting in a tent alone on the edge of the second biggest ice-cap in the world. My mind wandered. My neck and lips were agony, burned with the sun and the reflection off the snow. The boys' faces were scarlet, their beards significant already, Bill would soon be excellent for the cast of *Culloden* and Roger as the rogue in a smuggler film.

Roger dolloped a slab of butter into the frothing cocoa in the pan. We were off the sea ice and morale was high. It was Midsummer Day. Bill and I, at least, were more at home; we could face any mountaineering difficulty, but no more of that sinking to the knees at every second step. I was so comfortable in my sleeping-bag, and we went to bed at 7 p.m., intending to get up at twelve when we hoped for freezing snow. If the boat had left us at Edinburgh G.P.O. and our journey was to London we would just have reached Musselburgh—a sobering thought, after two days' marathon effort. At this rate, it would take us about a year!

* * *

Five hours sleep seems quite adequate when one is doing only physical work. I woke to the noise of Bill pumping up the primus. Was there a route up that rock? I crawled reluctantly out of the tent. There was a steely, silvery light about. God, it was cold. We loaded one sledge with three ration boxes and started to manhandle it up the snow wraith, twisting between the belts of rock. Suddenly Hugh bent down and picked up a pipe, full and ready to light! The Greenlanders' sledging route, after all! A little farther on Hugh stooped again and picked up a chewing-gum wrapping. Poor man, the only alternative when he found that he had lost his pipe. The route led us face to face with one rock wall after another, but there was always a way round. Then we could see a col above us, but the way to it was a steep snow gully with sheer walls. With four of us on the sledge we just managed to move, but it was backbreaking work.

Heave, haul, till I thought I would burst, then a few feet would be gained. Heave and on again. Above us, against crystal blue sky, was the outline of the col. My whole point in life was focused on reaching it. Up, up—suddenly a snow bunting burst into song. Joyfully, the fat little bird swooped across my vision, then up into the rocks twittering and trilling. We weren't alone in the world. I thought of the happy little wife squatting on her nest tucked safely away in a cranny, peering out at us with a beady eye.

We reached the col, and looked down on to a marvellous little frozen lochan. Beyond it was the curve of a gleaming glacier leading upwards, out of sight. A route! We galloped across the lake, and saw that the glacier looked easy, giving access to the Inland Ice. We deposited the load on a moraine boulder and turned back for the next. At the top of the gully, Roger threw himself on the sledge, Hugh followed suit, and they careered down at breakneck speed, riding it like a bronco. Bill and I ran, taking great leaps, till I lost my feet and zoomed down on my beam end. Another load and we graunched up again. The sun was now beating down, the snow was wetter and our job harder. My lips were sore, and this would make them worse. I kept smearing on more glacier cream and it smarted and stung like mad. Could we do it in four loads? None of us could face a fifth, and so the final one was enormous, but we set off from sea-level thankful that at last the expedition was "off the ground". Our highest point on the ice-cap would be 8,000–9,000 feet, so every foot gained was important. Every time I placed one foot above the other I thought with satisfaction that another few inches could be chalked off the list.

We could only just move the sledge. Roger heaved from behind. I felt suddenly frightened when I looked at the boys' faces, twisted and strained with the effort, sweating and tense. Bill's scarlet and Hugh's deathly pale. Experience and planning were nothing if we couldn't muster the physical strength. I hadn't got it; I had taken it for granted that the boys had. My

lips were agony. I was just about giving out when spurred on
again by the snow bunting. At last everything was at the lake.
Its surface was now slushy, and now and then one's foot went
through into nothingness. I was so hot I welcomed the icy cold
of the water. We all threw ourselves down on the moraine
boulders, letting the sun dry us out. It was glorious, as long as
we didn't have to work. It blazed down on me. I must spend
next summer on a hot beach with my children, I mused.
Strangely enough, our thermometer registered only 54°—my
face felt like 94°. I stirred and for the first time noticed the view.
We were perched on the glacier foot—at our feet, the little
magical lake, and below, the frozen fjord. The limit was
mountains. So many that they merged into each other, end-
lessly, up the coast of Greenland. Great boulders surrounded
us, chiselled off the cliff face by the frost. A pool of water
collected under each one, the snow being melted by reflection
from the rock. What an opportunity! I dug in the pots and
pans box for the soap, and peeled off my clothes. I left my bra
and pants soaking in one, my shirt and vest in another. A clean
rinse meant walking over to a new boulder.

"Don't be so extravagant," complained Hugh, "you're
polluting the water supply." But Roger and he followed suit
and soon the boulders were festooned with clothes already
looking the worse for wear. The whites were grey, and the greys
were off black.

We reappraised our equipment. We must cut the weight
down somehow. This morning's efforts had shown us how vital
this was if we were going to have the energy to reach the far side.
We had brought nylon bags to carry the food in, intending to
throw away the ration boxes when we reached the Inland Ice.
Now the time had come. I had filled any gaps in the boxes with
old newspapers when we had packed them in the spring. Now
they assumed the maddening attraction that old papers do
whenever one meets them, on the kitchen floor or round one's
chips. "How to smoke your own reindeer," I read out of one.
"Listen to this," shouted Roger, quoting from an account of a

trip into the forests of Poland. We pored over them mesmerised, exasperating Bill who was all for getting the job done.

Friends had helped us pack, and now various little presents came to light, slipped in without us knowing. I didn't let the others see me secreting a bottle of Drambuie into one bag of food supplies, meant to last for six days. When in the Antarctic Hugh had realised that man needs meat for energy, but this protein can be converted into energy only if wallowing in a sea of fat. In a cold environment one needs far more energy than when ticking over in a maritime climate. So our rations contained a high quantity of fat. Butter, margarine, cheese and milk. Hugh reckoned on 4,000 calories a day each, and a day's rations weighed two pounds a man. We had food for six weeks, so our weight for food alone was three hundred and fifty pounds. We could not cut this down but we attacked everything else. Hugh went into one of his "maniac" phases. He threw away the toothpaste, his stethescope, his leather camera case; he cut the edges off the maps, he buried the aerial photos, he tore the covers off his notebooks. I hastily hid the photos of the children in the pages of my diary, lest he insisted on jettisoning them too. We each had a small "personal" bag. Hugh's was practically empty and so was Bill's. Roger's and mine bulged. Anything of Roger's that we queried he insisted was vital either for his navigation or for mending the sledge.

I made a gallon of tomato soup and we drank it all, then lay down on top of our sleeping-bags at 3.30 p.m. "The glacier tomorrow," I thought, as I lay in the hot airless tent. My face radiated heat and my lips were sore. I never thought I'd be complaining of the heat on this expedition! The boys were snoring, especially Bill. I thought I heard the growl of a ptarmigan, and looked out of the open door. Nothing. Incredible how alone one can feel although surrounded by people, if they are asleep. I tried my book. I should have brought a more sophisticated one—Trollope would have been a good choice. Hugh was wearing an old pair of black pyjamas, and I suddenly saw a solution to my burnt face. I cut off a piece of sleeve and sewed on some tape at the corners to tie round my head. I made one for Hugh so that he couldn't complain about my attack on his pyjamas. Yashikomaks I called them, after our Japanese camera, and we lurked Easternly behind these masks as we loaded up half the load on one sledge and set foot on the glacier in the middle of the night.

The snow was crisp and we climbed up into a silent world. On and on, up and up, An Arctic explorer needs an endless capacity to keep going. Distances are so vast. Hugh and Roger argue that a polar man must have a great depth of character so as to keep slogging on. I wondered if an utter fool would not be better able to plod on and on, less likely to query the point of it all. The neat little paw marks of a fox track danced right across our path. What ever did it live on? I peered about, but could see nothing but the sides of the glacier bowl we were toiling up. There were some ominous black lines ahead. Crevasses. These are bound to form where the glacier bends off the plateau of the ice-cap and loses height to gain the sea. I was frightened of being swallowed up in a yawning gap thousands of feet deep, and prodded the ground ahead with my ice-axe before taking a step.

One huge crack cut right across our tracks. Bill and I were in front and we gingerly edged our way forward. We would have to cross it. Bill leapt over and I slithered my feet right to the edge before daring to jump. Then the sledge had to be handled across. Supposing it fell in. Its weight would drag us all after it. "Hold it—photo!" shouted Hugh, letting go of his end of the sledge as it was just at mid-point over the crevasse. Roger had a leg at either side. I was belaying the lot, holding the rope grimly across my shoulder, leaning on to my ice-axe with all my strength. Bill was clinging on to the bar front of the sledge, the "cow-catcher" as it was called, and now the job of holding the weight of four hundred pounds was on him.

More crevasses, but we were beginning to see over the rim of our glacier. A biting cold wind swept down, cutting through my shirt, but we couldn't stop here to put on anoraks. One final effort and we were over the top. Before us was nothing. Endless, endless distance—a sweep of white to the horizon. The Inland Ice.

A little rocky mount, or nunatak, was on our left and we anchored the loaded sledge beside it, tying it securely to some rocks. We wasted no time in turning our backs on the Inland Ice and hurrying back down towards the previous camp. Back down over the crevasses, then a glorious charge down the glacier descending 2,000 feet in one and a half hours.

"Celebration," announced Hugh and opened one little tin of gaffelbitter or pickled herring in a wine sauce, an Iceland delicacy adored by Hugh and I that he had secreted in his bag. My mouth watered as I waited for Hugh to lay mine out on my ration of biscuit. I sank my teeth into it—then clutched my face in agony. The sharp salty sauce had gone for my cracked lips. Tears of disappointment and pain seared my eyes.

I crawled into my sleeping-bag and re-read the letter from Nora Duff, the keeper's wife. Darling children! Surely Rona wasn't frightened of *all* the dogs. Robin was very strong for his age, although he had had pneumonia. He was two weeks old when he first accompanied us to Glencoe for a weekend's ski-ing in the Scottish hills and since then he had learnt to ski and swim and handle a canoe. Our relations foretold disaster and pneumonia from that first weekend, but we were actually staying in a luxurious hotel in Switzerland when he became ill. The standard of living had been too high and the central heating contrasted too much with the clear frosty air outside. If we had been as usual in a tent, all would have been well. Surely it wasn't a relapse of this? The Duffs would never have made the long journey into Lochgilphead unless things were bad.

Roger was busy as usual, turning the pages of his notebooks, whittling a rope, handling his sextant. We all threw out more belongings. I discarded the Eskimo pipe. One's idea of what's worth keeping is proportional to the distance one has to carry worldly goods. We all slept soundly in spite of the heat, knowing that tomorrow would see us and the loads at a height of 3,000 feet, on the edge of the Inland Ice.

V

Wʜᴀᴛ ᴀ ᴠɪᴇᴡ! I stood outside the tent, perched beside a little nunatak. We were 3,100 feet above the sea and all was well. There was an infinite stillness, a feeling of unrecorded time. And loneliness. Nothing was meant to live here. Nothing but us did. An Arctic desert. But now it was easier to go on than back. I could see the green of the frozen sea stretching out into the Denmark Strait, clutching Greenland in its paralytic grip. Mountains and mountains, up and down the coast. But we were turning our back on it all, and facing the empty west.

We had burned our boats and must reach the other side. How long would it take us? A fortnight? Could we average twenty miles a day? Darling children, I'm coming, I thought as we reorganised the loads and prepared for our first day's march. We were all excited and raring to go.

A sledge was to be jettisoned here. But would the over eight hundred pound load go on one sledge without breaking it? It looked fragile, a flimsy structure of runners and bridges, and weighed less than three pairs of Alpine skis. If it did break we'd be in the soup, as a man can carry only sixty to eighty pounds on his back for any length of time. Simple arithmetic showed that a man could not maintain himself for a journey of four hundred and fifty miles by what he could carry. But one can pull two hundred pounds on a sledge. A dog can pull only one hundred pounds, and also needs food. More dogs have to pull the sledge with the dog food, and so it goes on.

Along with the old sledge we abandoned here our old leather climbing boots and pulled on the gleaming white canvas "mukluks", saved from the Korean war. We left a jerrycan of paraffin as well and I could not bear to think of the waste as we built a cairn of snow on top of the unwanted sledge and left it at the edge of the last rocks on the east coastal range.

Life was to be simplified now to eating, working and sleeping.

How marvellous! But I couldn't be a peasant toiling my fields, or sledging on, for ever. I had to justify my physical effort with an intellectual reason, and Hugh's research programme satisfied this. I loved my electric blanket, automatic washing machine, deep pile carpets of home, but I needed the challenge of doing without. I needed to pit myself against the weather and terrain. I come alive with the wind in my hair and the mountains in front of me. I had still to find out if an ice-cap would do instead.

Roger balanced the four pairs of skis on top of the load on the sledge. The gradient would be too steep to wear them yet and so the sledge was at its heaviest. In fact, could we move it in a one-er or would we have to ferry the gear? Bill and I were to pull in the front, Roger and Hugh nearer the sledge. I pulled the green nylon harness over my head and hauled it down so that I would take the strain with my hips. It was 3 a.m. We were all in high spirits. We heaved on the sledge to get over its inertia. It moved forward and we were off.

My boots just gripped the snow as we marched jauntily up the easy gradient of the crest in front of us. Our direction was west. Bill being in front was the one with the compass. At his command we moved to the left or right, keeping on his course of 104°. The compass was not as infallible as we were used to, as the magnetic North Pole lies just off Greenland, in Baffin Island, resulting in the needle of our compass moving sluggishly many degrees off true. This discrepancy would increase the farther west we were.

The Inland Ice unfolded in front of us. It opened out into rolling downs as we came on to the plateau proper. Now we met the wind. It swept down, a blast of ice from the vastness of the North Pole. My yashmak froze, clanking against my chin like a slab of metal. Would my nose get frost bite? I pulled on my anorak hood, severing contact with Bill. One is never so alone as with a hood tied tightly round one's face. I could only see forward and there was nothing to see. It was like a white golf course, folds behind folds. We would get to the top of one, to find another. And so it would be again. How fast were we going—how far had we come? I couldn't talk to Bill. I was well aware now of the weight of the sledge. We were aiming for a snow col—how far away? Distance was impossible to judge. I couldn't be bothered to pull off my gloves to look at my watch. All my effort was needed now to pull the sledge.

Suddenly my rhythm was broken as Bill jerked on my rope. His feet had sunk through the surface. Then mine did, up to the knee. I hauled out my leg—two steps on the surface, then I broke through again, jolting and jerking my neck as the weight of the sledge came unevenly on my shoulders. Then we were floundering in deep soft, dry powder snow. A frightful effort to move the sledge. It kept tracking into our footsteps and grinding to a halt, its runners bogged down deep in the snow. Hugh and Roger heaved on the bamboo cow-catcher in front and Bill and I hauled on our harnesses. The sledge would move an inch and I would fall over. Getting up was like fighting out of a quicksand. Gasping for breath I glanced to the right and saw a glacier bending away down towards the sea, criss-crossed with bands of black lines—crevasses.

We were going downhill now, away from the glacier, and still it was the same. One step on the surface, another one. One's heart leapt—it was going to be all right, then crunch, up to the knee. Heave out, and again and again. How would we get to Søndre Strømfjord, four hundred miles away? A level of my mind dismissed this thought, but a lower level was in turmoil. The uncertainty of how deep my feet would sink was what was getting me. I began to despair. I glanced back and saw Roger and Hugh, heads down, heaving away calmly. Somehow this brought me up, and I took my weight on the rope once more. Now I knew what Hugh meant about polar travel being the ability to keep going on, and why he had often mooted the point that one needs to be well into one's thirties for a successful sledging trip. I had learnt this lesson in the Scottish hills, willing myself to slog on and on over a dreary moor in pouring

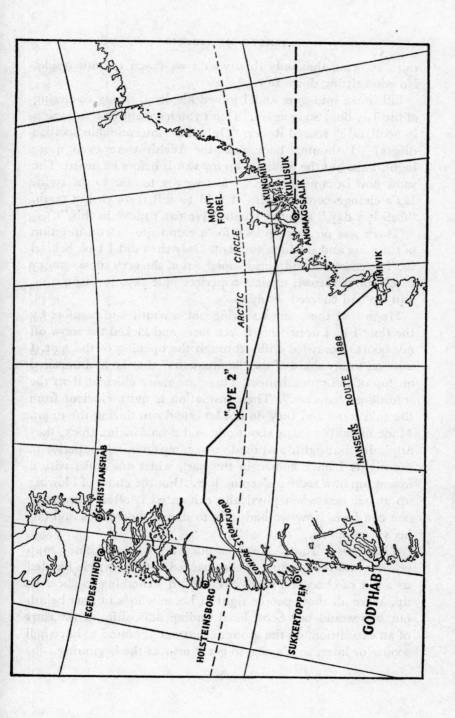

rain, knowing that only then would we reach the other side. No good sitting down to cry!

Bill broke into song and I joined his deep, strong rendering of the Tay Boat Song again. "Don't you have any cheerful songs in Scotland?" roared Roger. "Only these interminable Scottish dirges?" I shouted back that the Welsh were even more lugubrious, but the wind ate up my words before he heard. The snow now became deeper. "I feel we are too far to the right. Let's change course a bit," I said to Bill through my teeth. "Call it a day," shouted Hugh. "We can't move in this."

There was no need to look for a camp site—just a question of stopping and pitching the tent. Only then did I look behind us. The coastal mountains loomed out of the grey snow—rocky black spires thrown against a perfect blue sky. It was 9 a.m. and we had covered six miles.

Hugh had the primus roaring out warmth and comfort by the time I had untied my frozen laces and kicked the snow off my boots. I crawled stiffly through the opening of the tent. I sank on to my share of the "kampamats" that he had unrolled on top of the ground sheet. These are more efficient than the traditional "air bed". Their insulation is more efficient from the cold snow and they do not let one down during the night. Made of rubber foam about one and a half inches thick, they are bulky but light, and made our camp infinitely superior to the nights I have known in the past, when one woke with a frozen hip or a sodden sleeping bag. Also, the chore of blowing up an air bed when physically exhausted is often more than one can face. Now we had only to unroll these mats, and our beds were made.

"Home is a Tent." Hugh emptied a packet of kidney soup powder into the pressure cooker packed with snow. He handed us a bar of chocolate each—we needed something to cheer us up. Were all those people right at home who said how hellish our trip would be? Scott liked finding difficulties at the start of an expedition, on the grounds that one is bound to have hell sooner or later, so it's nice to get it over at the beginning.

Roger thrives on difficulties. As others sink, his enthusiasm rises. Fortified by a gallon of soup, he was bounding with energy. "Let's go for a recce. Perhaps we are too far to the right, into the upper reaches of that glacier—the surface may be fine farther left. But you stay here," he said to me, meeting my unenthusiastic face, "we don't all need to go."

How marvellous to be by myself! But as soon as the boys were out of sight I felt ridiculously lonely. I also felt in need of a good wash. I melted a panful of snow and set to work. My face was peeling off in shreds and the soap stung my lips, but I was purring with self-satisfaction by the time I had finished.

I then set about making supper and scooped the pressure cooker full of snow once more. I threw two handfuls of onions on top and waited for the snow to melt. Our ration of dried meat was 4 oz. each per day, so I broke up the blocks and dropped them in. I threw in a slab of marge to keep up with Hugh's ideas of fat intake, and a squeeze of Marmite to pep up the taste. Although there is only one way to make "dehy stew", it tastes completely different when made by someone else. When the others returned it was bubbling like an Icelandic pool of volcanic mud. "Too far to the right," said Hugh, but I got no opportunity to say "I told you so". We slurped up our stew and slithered into our bags, all quite sure that tomorrow would see us really on our way. I fell asleep to the sound of Roger and Hugh talking. They were on to their usual subject of who reached the North Pole first. They agreed that the American, Peary, did not, but this did not stop them from discussing the subject again and again and again.

"The thing is," said Roger, "if he really did reach the pole on April 7th and camp 87° 47' on the 9th, he had to travel 150 miles in two days—those positions are quite definite in his book. He just couldn't do that speed."

"Macmillan once did a hundred miles in a day with dogs," said Hugh.

"Yes, but that was in ideal racing conditions, not over the very rough polar pack and with leads to cross. Remember, he

79

was a man of 53, far beyond his prime, and he was wearing thick furs."

Hugh asked, "What about Peary's other journeys—did he ever manage these speeds?"

"No, that's the whole point; on his ice-cap crossings he only managed twenty or so miles a day."

"But the trouble is, if you're going to shoot a man down for this you have to be absolutely certain," said Hugh.

"What makes me certain," said Roger, "is that he said to the Congressional Committee that he didn't use skis or ride on the sledge, and when challenged he could only manage twenty-nine miles walking in a day on the excellent roads in Washington D.C.!"

"Yes," said Hugh, "anyone who's done any dog sledging at speed knows you must ride or use skis—that clinches it as far as I'm concerned. It's extraordinary that he's on every map and atlas as the conqueror of the North Pole."

"Yes," said Roger, "that beats me too. I'm looking forward to scrutinising his diaries when they're published. The trouble I think is that there was too much vested interest in his success. The whole thing's a bit of a farce anyway—the Eskimoes who accompanied him kept looking for a hole in the ground."

*　　　*　　　*

I slipped my skis forward one after the other, and on and on. There was nothing to see ahead except the sky. I had never been aware of it so much before. I became excited now when a cloud formed and slipped across that vast expanse of blue. I knew it would break up my monotony by throwing a shadow on the snow. Sometimes two or three played together. The only noise was the sledge grinding over the snow, lumbering along behind. I had nothing to do but haul and think. I had to think to think of something to think about. But I couldn't think deeply, just on the chit-chat level to occupy my mind. I spent two days thinking of a holiday lying in the sun and another designing a new house. Time dragged interminably on. Should I eat my chocolate now? I'll keep it another half hour. No, I can't. I slipped one hand out of its glove and got out the little bar. Was it nuts today? Or plain? Hurray, it was nuts. My searching fingers felt the bumps. I tore off the silver paper with my fingers still deep in my pocket and broke the bar into bits. Little bits. I laughed when I once heard my Bruce tell Rona to break her Easter egg into little bits, as it would go farther if she did. Now I took his advice and did the same.

Nectar! I slipped a piece of chocolate into my mouth and my teeth crunched on the nuts. Saliva drooled into my mouth and too soon it was gone. But I had another piece! My glove came off again to pop in the next square.

Roger always hoarded his chocolate, never feeling the craving that I had to gobble it up at once. Hugh never kept his, but ate it at once, as soon as it was dished out, then forgot all about it and never regretted his hasty act. Bill decided at what time he would eat his and never altered course, never succumbed to temptation and ate it before time, or forgot it and had it late. I was the only one with no self-discipline, the only one green with greed.

At least now we were breaking one mile per hour. The snow was more consolidated and our skis met less resistance on the surface. We had crossed the Border in my mental journey from Edinburgh to London. We wore our skis now as one normally did a pair of boots. Without them we would sink up to the waist in the snow. Ours were light-weight cross-country Norwegian planks, plastic soles and an edge of harder wood. The bindings were loose, giving the maximum heel lift, gripping the boot only at the toe. It gave me tremendous satisfaction actually to use the skis rather than play with them on the slopes beside a ski tow.

Every three hours Roger called us to a halt. Thankfully I would collapse, leaning over my ski sticks. There was nowhere to sit down. Roger would pull out his meteorological notebook and write his observations of the weather. "That's where my biro went," Bill would accuse. Roger would answer with one of his smiles and put it back again into his pocket. He never entered into an argument. He measured the temperature by a whirling psychrometer—a thermometer attached to a universal joint. It always read low when I was dying of heat and high on the days that I could have cried with the cold. We all held our breath while he then went back to look at the milometer. How far had we gone since the last stop? The importance of this assumed enormous significance. Already it was the last week in June. We had three hundred miles still to go and we must arrive in early August. We were just as interested in the altimeter. Our chosen route should take us over a col no higher than 8,500 to 9,000 feet. If we had to climb higher we had made a mistake. We were now at 4,700—higher at least than anyone at home, I thought with satisfaction. The longing to stop was nearly equalled by the longing to get moving again before the icy winds froze my blood. How I hated the wind, always against me, battering at my face, whipping up anything I put on the ground, throwing ice crystals into my eyes, tearing at my hair.

I noticed now that the sky was not as limitless as usual, a ceiling of cloud was creeping in. Soon it swallowed up the sun. We pressed on into a greying world that became smaller and smaller as the mists stole up around us. Snow began to fall. We stumbled forward blindly. Bill held the compass in his hand and checked it every few minutes, but even so we often swayed 90° off course. I lost my sense of balance. Was I going uphill or down? I thought I had stopped, and fell over still moving. I had to force myself not to panic. We couldn't get lost with a compass, a sextant and an altimeter—or could we? Suddenly, I nearly jumped out of my skin. A big white fox with a black face was leaping frantically about the snow, just within sight. "It must have followed us all the way from the land," I thought, overcome with guilt. It bounded towards us, shied like a horse, then shot off into the mist, jumping high to free its feet from the snow. It was gone. We were alone once more.

I could understand now how Scott died only ten miles from his depot. I knew now the effort of battling on, the hard won tenths of a mile, the personal fight against just sitting down in the comfortable enveloping snow.

Time for Roger's "ob." again. Thankfully I saw Hugh untying the tent. "What's this," said Roger, "stopping? Let's clock off another three miles." I was far too tired to put my weight to an argument. It was easier to go on. But soon the snow turned to sleet. We couldn't afford to get wet to the skin, and then use up several day's paraffin to dry out the clothes. In a few moments I was inside the tent, leaving Roger as usual to unravel the harnesses, stand up the skis, pile snow on the valance of the tent and unscrew the milometer before it froze.

It was lovely in the tent, warm and safe, even though we were in the midst of nowhere. Wet snow slapped against the walls. Two thin layers of nylon separated us from hell.

"Leave your nose alone," I shouted at Hugh as I saw him finger a piece of loose skin and shred it off, leaving pinheads of blood on the raw surface. "I love to be weak," he said with relish as he felt around for some more. I resisted following suit, feeling the pain that would result.

Curried meat-bar stew with three handfuls of onions, followed by ice-cream of milk powder and snow. Delicious. I sank back against the sleeping-bag to read. I had my hand at last on Roger's "Memoirs". They satisfied me completely, sophisticated and civilised. Roger himself was poring over his almanac and charts. Hugh studied his urines—what secrets were his test tubes going to unfold? Were we going to churn out the same amount of hormone all the way across or would our glands become accustomed to the physical effort and revert to normal? I cursed Hugh every time I participated in the experiment. It was all very well for the boys to use a bottle—extraordinarily difficult for me. He was furious at the loss of a drip but he was only one that made the mistake of once using someone else's bottle. Nor did he think it funny while we roared with laughter at his lapse.

Rain lashed the tent all night and throughout the next day. It was marvellous to wake up, listen, and snuggle back down into the two layers of sleeping-bag again. There was no decision to be made—no question of moving on in that. Rain was the one contingency we had not expected to meet on the Greenland ice-cap; we might as well have been camping in Glencoe. We slept for six hours and woke to make porridge, slept for another six and awoke for soup. After another six hours I had enough energy for a game of chess. Bill was filling the pressure cooker with snow. "Washing?" I asked. "Yes, my underpants," said Bill. Our hurrahs exploded over the ice-cap but our joy was shortlived. They looked the same after as before. "There will be a freeze-up tonight," foretold Hugh as he arranged his pawns for another game of chess. Sure enough, light was creeping back into the sky by the early hours of the morning; the grey of the snow was separated from the grey of the sky by a thin line. The tent walls were creaking. We could go on again.

It was bitterly cold. I could not bear the moment when we dismantled the tent and destroyed our haven of warmth and life. Solid slabs of ice were clinging to the tent. Bill and I beat at them with our ice axes before we could fold it back into its bag. At last the sledge was loaded and we lined up for the big heave. It wouldn't move!

"Iced up," Hugh diagnosed, starting to undo the work of the last hour without complaint. I stood stock-still, frozen stiff. Bill dug a hole and crouched in it while the others pulled the sledge over his head. He chipped at the runners and at last they were satisfied with the result and loaded up again. The sledge leapt into action behind us and our skis slithered over the glazed surface. Now the boot was on the other foot; we could get no traction to enable us to pull on the sledge. Another stop. Hugh had the idea of tying rope around the skis under our boots. Reluctantly we cut strips off the climbing rope; it seemed to work.

One step forward, half a step back. The sun had rolled back

the clouds and was glittering on the new snow crystals, making them fairy-tale, shimmering stars. The sky was red, a magic world as we stopped five hours later for Roger to take a sextant reading to check up on our course after the storm. The radio was unpacked and we crowded round the sledge. The strains of "Lilliburlero" proved that we were tuned in to the B.B.C. We waited for the critical pips. No one had ever taught me the relationship between time and distance before. "If my calculations are right," announced Roger, "we have a hundred and sixty-four miles to go to that U.S. Dew line station—or isn't there one?" "I hope they have some fresh milk," I thought. "Steaks for me," drooled Roger. "Chicken Maryland," said Hugh. "Corn fritters and banana." From now on, at every stop Roger told us the altitude, the temperature and the distance to "Chicken Maryland", our new name for the American base.

The wind freshened, blowing a layer of spindrift that completely covered our skis. It was an eerie, peculiar world—as if nothing had been here before us or ever would again. The wind tore at my scarlet cagoul—a nylon smock used in addition to our anoraks. God, I was cold! I had all my clothes on too. My vest was of pure wool, a cast-off of my brother-in-law, who had given it to my mother to sell at a jumble sale. He had got it from his father, so it dated from the days when what looked like wool was wool, no question of nylon mixtures. (I hate string vests. I always get caught up in the holes, nor am I convinced of their warmth over traditional wool.) I then wore a thin, soft cashmere polo-necked jersey, old with the elbows out; on top of this a "Vyella" shirt. We had each been given two by the manufacturers, long cosy tails to tuck in, plenty of room to move, yet neat at the neck and cuff. They were a subdued tartan, easy on the eye. Two or three layers of thin wool are far warmer than one thick and also far more comfortable than a heavy double knit. My top layer was another jersey, straight from the Hawick mills, mine and Bill's a bottle green, Hugh's and Roger's a seal grey. They were light, yet as warm as wool could be. I also wore "long johns" of a nylon mixture, hugging my legs and thighs, with wind-proof trousers on top. These were two layers of nylon and cotton weave, in a bright and cheerful blue. I padded out my mukluks with a pair of sea-boot stockings under two felt socks, and my feet and legs were never cold when dry, in spite of the wind. Roger wore no underclothes and seldom his jersey, yet never once complained of the cold. He was as thin as a rake, and ate less than Bill, but somewhere had stowed away an inner fire of energy and enthusiasm that kept him warm.

Gloves were a problem. Really warm mittens of fur would have been too clumsy for undoing ski bindings and tying on the loads to the sledge. Yet fingered gloves were too cold. I wore a thin wool pair under leather mitts, but my hands froze when I took off the outer layer, and sweated with it on.

In the tent we were too hot and our sleeping-bags too efficient for the temperatures that we experienced. I usually lay on top, but then I missed the security and comfort of being snuggled up to the chin.

We struggled against the wind, through the animated spindrift, whirling and twisting over our feet and hiding our skis. Roger's ob. came round again. I could have cried with the cold. It took four of us to pitch the tent in the tearing wind that whipped the canvas out of our hands as it screamed around our heads. At last I was inside. But could I bear the pain when my hands came back to life? "Eighty miles to the top," said Roger, as we poured scalding tomato soup into our frozen bodies. Then we slept that marvellous sleep that comes only to really exercised muscles. The next day was my birthday. I remembered this as Bill stirred the porridge at 4 p.m. In our upside down world, tomorrow came at lunch time and we ate oatmeal for supper. I quickly sat up and reached for the nylon bag with powdered milk. The greatest luxury in my world was the froth that collected on top when the powder was stirred into warm water. Only the mixer was allowed to lick this, and Hugh and I vied with each other for the job, but no one else admitted that they hankered after it as much as I. Hugh was lining up the biscuits, four each, with a sliver of butter and a squeeze of black Marmite. He didn't put the lid back on quick enough, and he cursed as it oozed down the tube and over his fingers, a sticky gooey mess. Bill, as usual, was trying to hurry us up. He had already rolled up his sleeping-bag and was now struggling to get a kampamat out of the door. Difficult, as Roger was still sitting on half of it, and had his innumerable notebooks scattered all about.

Hugh dished out the porridge. My helping was half the size of the boys. The sugar bag was almost empty but we didn't start a new ration bag for another day. One had to last six. I was tempted to break into a new one and "borrow", but Hugh was always horrified at the suggestion. I dolloped an extra large nut of margarine into my bowl. Oily yellow bubbles broke the surface and joined with the froth of the milk. Delicious!

"Go halves on a tea bag, Roger?" I asked, having drained my first cup and longing for a second. I dunked the little bag up and down in my mug of boiling water, then transferred it to Roger's, splashing Hugh with hot water as I did so. Hell! I pulled the string too hard and the bag exploded in his cup. Soggy tooth-catching leaves floated in a solid mass to the top. "Look at that garbage," said Hugh, but Roger drank it without complaint.

I still found it difficult to start the day's work at 5 p.m. How marvellous it would be to sleep all night. I pulled on my sea-boot stockings over my long johns of pale blue and unpinned my mukluks from where they dangled from the roof of the tent. Every time I laced them up I cursed the fact that all Korean soldiers had such enormous feet. I was always last out of the tent. I had an unconscious reluctance to take it down and expose myself to the naked vastness of the surroundings. We seemed so much more vulnerable without it.

When I did put my head out I was dazzled with the sun. I stepped on to the snow and sank into the wet slushy surface. Something squeaked. I was flabbergasted. There it was again. I looked up. There were four terns, whiter than white,

87

quivering their forked tails against the pale blue sky. Rising and falling, chattering together. We had captured their attention, and we focused ours on them. So alive, their swooping movements thrilled me. Then they were off, rising up into the sky as if on a string, till they were absorbed into the limitless blue.

I slipped my gross mukluked feet into my ski bindings, and my hands through the loop of my sticks. "Two, four, six," yelled Roger and we heaved with all our might to get the sledge on the move. The surface was slushy even though it was 5 p.m., but as soon as we got going I cut off contact with the outside world and sank into my daydreams again. As the sun crept down in the sky the surface hardened up, and suddenly we found ourselves zooming along. Time sped too. A warm feeling of satisfaction crept over me as my body moved to the rhythm. Stick in, foot forward, thrust with your shoulders, other foot on. We bit into the distance—I felt it rolling away under my skis. The sun appeared to come nearer and hovered on the horizon, a red three-dimensional, round disc, throwing a golden glow on the snow and a radiance into the sky. The world was a marvellous place, and as my skis moved effortlessly on, my thoughts were drowned in the pleasure of physical rhythmical movement. Stopping for Roger's met. ob. became a nuisance. I wanted to go on and on and on.

But the sun slipped below the rim of our white saucer and immediately our world was God forsaken, icy cold and deathly white. Hugh called us to a stop. It was midnight and we had covered ten whole miles. I held the end of the nylon bag while Bill and Hugh pulled out the tent, then we each took a leg and stood it up on the snow, fighting the wind that flapped the canvas in our faces. We threw in a bedding roll each to sit on, the primus box and the currant-red nylon food bag. I scooped the pressure cooker full of snow and put it on to melt. Oxtail soup. We sat round licking our lips, too tired to talk till it was ready. At last thick brown bubbles broke the surface and Hugh slopped it out into our four plastic bowls. "Had no one else remembered that it was my birthday?" I thought. I looked at Hugh but he was concentrating on his soup. I longed to be alone with him, able to talk without the others being there, but he didn't seem to feel the same. We shared a double sleeping-bag but that was all. Suddenly I felt full of self-pity and hated the three men sitting round the tent. I couldn't bear Bill's red bristly beard or Hugh's peeling nose. I cringed at Roger's missing front tooth. My eyes met his. "Happy birthday," he said with his enormous grin. It was July 5th and I could not bear it.

Soon we were off again. The sun was just back in the sky and the surface hard and crisp. The sledge sped on. With my anorak hood up I wallowed in my self-pity as I had in my teens.

We were beating the clock. "More than 2 m.p.h." shouted Roger next time he looked at the wheel. We leaned on our long sticks to propel us forward and our skis swept over the surface. I had the impression of a steep bank in front that we never quite reached. Some clouds on the left looked like icebergs in the sea but the mirage melted as the sun stalked up into the sky. I could have gone on for ever—until the surface began to melt and clutch at our plastic soles.

"Hold it," said Hugh and I straightened up. Suddenly I was tired. I stepped out of my skis and dropped my harness on the ground. I couldn't even carry it back to the sledge and hardly helped put up the tent on the flat pan of hard snow just the size for our site. I pulled a kampamat out of its bag and pushed it through the entrance, longing to collapse on top. But first I had to take off my boots and brush away the snow. . . . The jobs seemed endless. Bill was on his kampamat before me, digging in his bag. "Here," he said and tossed me two bars of chocolate that landed by my side. "Oh Bill," was all I could say. Tears stung my eyes. Chocolate was gold to us. I felt awful for hating Bill earlier in the day. Roger put a box down in the middle of the tent: Black Magic. I could hardly wait to sink my teeth into a crunchy, nutty coffee centre. With a shout of triumph Hugh produced a tin of gaffelbitters and one of cock-tail nuts.

What a feast! We demolished the lot. Hardly keeping our eyes open while we munched the last mouthful of nuts. . . .

I woke peculiarly satisfied and content. My sleeping-bag was so comfortable I could hardly bear to stir. I found a nut lurking in a tooth and turned it over in my mouth, savouring its delight.

"Look what I've found," said Bill and I knew that he was referring to the bottle of Drambuie secreted in one of the food bags by a good friend at home. "This calls for ice-cream," said Hugh so I tipped the last of the cocoa tin into a bowl of snow and stirred in some dried milk. "Great discovery," shouted Roger, "another layer of Black Magic hidden in the box." The warm glow of the whisky filled me with love for everything, even Bill's beard.

A ground mist crept up as we loaded up the sledge. Soon we were enveloped in a damp, clammy fog but the miles ticked by. I kept looking over my left shoulder. I had a curious feeling that there was someone else there—the Green Man of Greenland, obviously a relation of the Grey man of Macdhui at home, who stalks after any climbers out on his hill on a misty day, particularly if they are alone. Footsteps are heard in the snow, which quicken as one hurries to get away, and yet the Grey Man is said to be quite friendly, and some climbers have enjoyed his company as they have strode down the heathery slopes towards the pass of the Lairig Ghru that cuts through the great Cairngorms of central Scotland.

This Green Man was not frightening either, but I felt annoyed that he kept hidden in the grey wraiths of mist. I kept expecting something to loom up out of the mist in front too. Bill confessed that he felt the same and expected a tree or a hedge. Roger said that he had the impression we were walking in a groove with steep banks on either side but knew about the Green Man too. The mist muffled the limitless world, giving us a secret place of retreat, or as if we were travelling in a sort of box, or perhaps a sedan chair.

*　　　*　　　*

8,150 feet on the altimeter—when will it start to drop? We must be nearly at the col. Ten miles went by. It was misty again but a glint of sun threw life on to the snow. "Hey," said Roger, "it's only 8,050 on the clock!" We all straightened up. A thrill of excitement spread through me. "Do another few miles to make sure," said Hugh, but he was as excited as us.

Instead of retreating into my anorak hood I chatted to Bill of experiences we had shared through the years. "Remember that weekend we stayed in the bothy at the foot of Creag Meaghaidh? It lashed with rain." We rambled on about "the time we cooked our supper on burning grass as someone had forgotten the primus, and then lost the summit of Ben à Bhuird in the moonlight". We recalled a marathon ascent of Ben Cruachan from a camp in Glencoe. "Remember we hitch-hiked back in a brand new car with white seat covers and we were oozing mud and rain? Remember the smell as the heater started to work on your anorak?"

I was taken by surprise when the sledge rumbled to a halt. I looked back to see Hugh and Roger taking off their skis. We ate our supper sitting outside the tent, the primus burning merrily in the unexpected calm. The air was balmy. The boys peeled off their shirts and I was suddenly struck with the urge to wash. The temperature was 31°. "Forty-five miles to Chicken Maryland," said Roger, as I took his sextant from him and twisted the mirror so that I could see my face. Heavens, was that me? Scarlet nose, deeply lined face, blisters on each cheek, bloated eyelids, dank hair, cracked lips. No wonder Hugh didn't love me! Bill was fiddling with the wireless. Suddenly an Anglo-Indian voice burst out, "Come to Wales for your holidays," it urged. Roger glowed with satisfaction, although he hadn't spent a holiday there for more than fifteen years; "You won't regret it." I got out my writing things, to be ready with a despatch if Chicken Maryland did materialise, but when it came to the point I didn't want to put this private world of ours on paper to be read by masses on the Blackpool beach. Instead I gazed at the children's photos. I could hear Rona's squeaky voice. "I so tired I need clockclick," was her current phrase, believing chocolate to cure all ills. Bruce's last words still rang in my ears, "See you in Greenland, Mum," he had shouted cheerfully, his little monkey face sparkling with excitement. My thoughts lingered on Robin, the one old enough to miss us most. "Couldn't I come too?" he had said; "I'm good in blizzards you know." And so he was. I remembered a particular trip last winter when we had camped near the top of the ski tow in the Cairngorms to test the new Arctic tent. Five-year-old Robin had left the tent and skied down for a "last run". The weather deteriorated to such an extent that the tow was closed before Hugh could bring him back up. By then a full scale blizzard was raging, drifting, blinding snow, and the wind too strong for a "piggy back". They floundered through deep drifts, and Robin only complained when a reindeer loomed out of the gathering darkness and put its front feet on his shoulders, sending him sprawling on the snow. They arrived at the tent with their eyelashes iced up to their hair. Icicles dangled from Robin's chin and his hands were stiff. His fat cheeks turned scarlet as they thawed out, once he was stuffed into a sleeping-bag in the safe, warm tent, but he was out again the next day, quite prepared to battle again.

Another "day". The tent was the most desirable place until the sleeping-bags were rolled away and one's few belongings pushed back into the nylon sacks. Then the naked groundsheet was cold and uncomfortable and I wanted to be off as quickly as we could. Our world was always different when I crawled out of the tent. This time it was misty but the sun was there like a light bulb through a piece of paper. There was a darker line around it. "Sign of frost," said Roger knowingly. I looked upon my skis now as I would a pair of shoes. They were part of our life. I pulled the harness over my head and clipped on the trace joining it to the sledge. One big pull and it started at once. The going was easy and the sledge purred along behind on the silky snow. We took it for granted now that we could cover three miles per hour. Roger wanted a time check at 10 G.M.T., but instead of longing for the stop, I was sorry. Bill fixed up the aerial while Hugh fiddled with the knobs of the little wireless. Suddenly, a voice we knew boomed out—the Scottish Overseas Programme—and the militant beat of "Scotland the Brave" thrust itself into our world. "Land of the high endeavour, Land of the purple heather," roared Bill at the top of his powerful voice, joining in the song. Suddenly I wanted to cry. We looked so silly, standing round the tiny sledge that carried all our defences for survival against the vast, hostile world completely surrounding us and stretching for eternity. One turn of the knob and we were alone again and I felt more complete. The endless wind had whipped up the surface now into "sastrugi", like beaten white of egg. Sastrugi are drift-like formations in the snow caused by wind and snow erosion. These carve up the surface, leaving behind these ridges which may be three feet or more in height. The word is Russian and makes me think of the endless wind howling across Siberia, blasting those vast distances with snow and sand, whittling down the surface and driving everyone mad. I had to concentrate, to watch my feet so as not to trip over and land with a thud, bruising my legs on the edge of my ski. The sledge rode along now like a Victorian carriage, twisting to accommodate the irregularities of the ground. Now I knew why ours was lashed together and not nailed. It was like the articulated wooden crocodile my children once had, that writhed along behind them on a piece of string,

Roger was right, the night became colder and the atmosphere clear. I straightened up and looked on towards the horizon. "Hey!" I shouted and stopped. "What's up?" asked Bill, annoyed at the break in the rhythm. "I can see something," I said, but now I wasn't so sure. Perhaps it was a particularly large sastrugi a few feet away. We were so unused to seeing anything vertical on our flat desert of white that my eyes were not orientated to a change.

We went on again, but I was mesmerised by that black "blob". It wasn't sastrugi. "Chicken Maryland!" I suddenly shouted, absolutely convinced.

Hugh climbed on to the sledge and peered, and so did Roger. They agreed. There certainly was "something". But should we change course and go to it? It was 15 degrees to our left. Supposing it was only—only what? What could it be but Chicken Maryland?

We set off with the sun strangely on our right. The hours ticked by and so did the miles. The solid object on the horizon grew larger and more definite, then faded, appeared again, vanished, came into sight once more. What on earth was it? Our skis pounded over the creaking snow. We had covered ten miles and it seemed no nearer. "I think it's a helicopter crash," said Roger, "about twelve miles away." "I think it's two miles off, and it's petrol drums left by the French 1955 expedition," I said. "It's a food dump left by Paul Emil Victor, full of wine and camembert," insisted Hugh. Bill, stoic as ever, plodded on regardless. "Whatever it is, its twenty-four miles at least." Another two hours passed. "It's a Russian Church," I shouted suddenly, recognising the odd domed appearance. Occupied by the Russians or was it the cardboard set-up for a James Bond film? Had we been seen? Our tracks must have shown up for miles. Perhaps only robots lived there, pro-grammed to turn a ray gun on all boarding parties as they approached.

"Speed up," urged Hugh. "We must get there before the thaw sets in." Only then did I realise that it was 7 a.m. We had been going for twelve hours since seeing "it" first, twenty-four miles ago. "I'll have to stop—I'm so hot and thirsty," I tried to complain, but the boys were off again and I had to struggle to keep up. But we could see now what we were heading for. My impression was of a dome, perched on a black metal box, with black legs supporting it above the snow. Extra hemispheres, faceted like gigantic half golf balls, were attached to the sides. A sort of cat-walk ran around the top. Figures were moving on it! We waved our ski sticks and shouted, like shipwrecked men shrieking from their desert island at a passing ship. The figures disappeared. "They've gone to get their snow tractors to come and meet us," I thought with confidence. Little flags now came into view, dotted about in the snow. An air strip! We came to a halt at the edge of it and gazed, flummoxed, at the weirdest contraption James Bond or anyone else ever saw.

The fantastic science fiction erection towered above us, its engines throbbing out a deadly life. No one came out. Had no one seen us after all? "Some early warning system this," I thought indignantly. "Let's blow it up," suggested Roger, his blue eyes twinkling at the thought.

What do to next? Where was the front door to knock on? I felt rather rude, barging in on the place with all our goods and chattels, like stumbling upon someone bathing in the nude, convinced of their seclusion.

"Leave the sledge here," pronounced Hugh and we all stepped out of our traces. "Careful," Hugh warned as we started to cross the runway, and we all looked apprehensively up and down as if faced with the traffic in Sauchiehall Street. A yellow caterpillar tractor was moving to and fro, shovelling snow. It drove underneath the building, and I suddenly appreciated how enormous the erection was. The tractor passed easily right underneath. I followed suit as the boys freed their feet from their skis, and started to walk towards it. Was the driver blind? He passed right in front of me. I waved. He waved and drove on! Suddenly I was frightened. A vision of being run over and ground into the snow flashed through my mind. I started to run over to Hugh, stumbling over the rutted caterpillar tracks. My heart was pounding, and I felt faint and awfully sick. Hugh was talking to a man outside a shed. I sat down on an oil drum and held my head in my hands. Oh to be alone, I thought, meaning the four of us in our little tent. The noise of engines thudded through my head. I needed this man-made horror to show me the marvellousness of our world on the Inland Ice. The virgin, gleaming snow sweeping on to meet the clear blue sky that stretched out above us, dotted with endless variations of white feathery cloud. The feeling of being self-sufficient and part of the scene gave one enormous satisfaction—a sort of glow as one watched the sun creep up to meet the moon. The crispness of the night frost that made the snow squeak beneath our ski. The golden glory as the sun sank behind a belt of cloud poised on the horizon, spilling gilt and scarlet on to the snow. The feeling of absolute confidence in Bill and Roger, who I knew would never let me down or complain if I did not pull the sledge as hard as they did, who would see the journey through whatever lay in our path.

The caterpillar driver was still driving, Roger and Bill stood awkwardly by my side. Hugh was talking to the man, with his "withdrawn" look on his face, a sign of an infuriating situation. "No, we haven't crashed our plane, we walked here," I heard him say in a cool, calm, icy voice, while the man looked as if he had met a flock of lunatics and chewed frantically on his gum. He went into the shed and picked up a phone. "Contacting the main building," explained Hugh. "God, I feel awful," I moaned weakly, looking for sympathy. "You can't be sick here," was all I got.

"They say you can't come in until they have permission from the authorities in Washington," drawled our man, while I gazed fascinated at his jaws working on the gum.

I felt hostile, my reaction to being unwanted. I stood up, mastering my dignity and any flecks or aristocracy. "Never mind," I said in my most withering voice, "we will just go on."

But suddenly, something happened. People spilled out of the building, clicking the cameras that dangled round every neck. They pushed us into a group; more photos. They shook our hands, freezing for an instant for the scene to be immortalised on the hard-worked film. I shook hands with one man twice. "Once more for the folks," he said, pommelling my hand yet again. "Oh, wrong exposure," so we started from scratch once more. Everyone was enveloped in enormous fur-lined jackets, with white faces showing as little area as possible to the light of the sun. I, in a shirt, was dying of heat.

We were propelled now to the bottom of a ladder disappear-

Over the inland ice

Crossing a melt-stream on the west side of the ice-cap

Melt-stream technique

A camp during the descent

Discovery of beer-cans: Roger, Myrtle and Bill

The East Coast:
Carsten Berg-
Sørensen

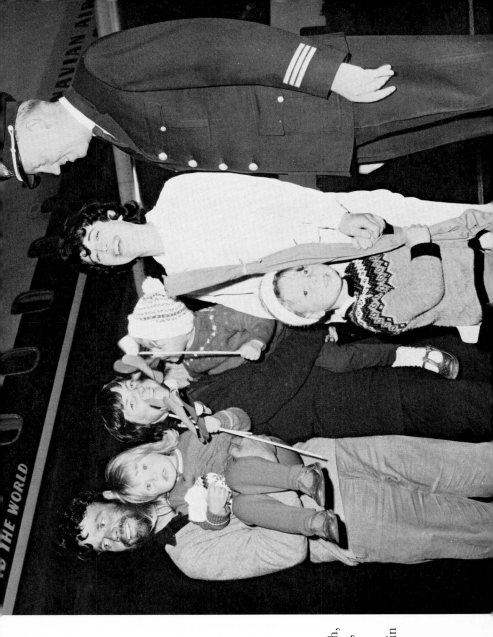

Meeting the children: Hugh, Rona, Myrtle, Bruce, Robin and Heather; with the captain of their plane

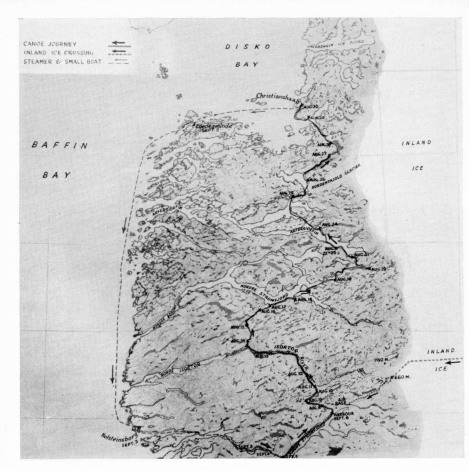

Map of canoe route

ing into the maw of the building. "Welcome to Dye 2," was carved on the first rung. People were crowding behind; I had to go up, then over the drawbridge. It was like a ship inside, and we followed a dark metal corridor till it spread out into a canteen. Oranges! I saw a pile of them, large and shining. My fingers itched to tear off the skin and sink my teeth into the mouth-watering juicy flesh.

"What would you like? Coffee?" asked everyone. "Fresh bread," said Roger speaking for us all. A platter of enormous doorstep sandwiches was put in front of us, and cups of black coffee, plus a little packet marked "instant cream". A large cream cake was added to our table, but all we wanted was the bread. We munched into crisp fresh lettuce, wedges of tomato and slices of Spam, encased in the delicious texture of bread.

Everyone talked at once, leaning over us, pushing to get close, the cameras still working hard. The general theme was that "no one has ever arrived here on foot before—let alone a dame!" Roger and Hugh explained and described the expedition, but I suddenly realised as I looked round at the faces that they had no real idea of our journey. None of them went outside except to board a plane. They were completely insulated from all contact with their environment. This Little America could have been anywhere.

I turned the conversation on to them. Dye 2 was called after the master station at Cape Dyer on Baffin. It was maintained by the American Air Force stationed at Søndre Strømfjord, who flew in fresh meat and mail twice a week. The men here were all civilians working for the Federal Electric Corporation on contract for the U.S. Government, at a salary of several hundred a week. "Dollars?" I said, never knowing how to work the rate of exchange in my head. "No, pounds," was the answer.

"Want a bath?" asked the crew-cut boss. It was an obvious question, I thought, glancing round at the boys' peeling faces and scruffy beards. And yet it was the clean hygienic Americans I felt a revulsion from, with their smooth baby faces and scented hair. A young lad who said he was the chief radar technician ushered me up several flights of stairs, till we must have been at the level of the "radar works". "Lead Redition" was on the door of his room. He showed me in, handed me a new towel, swept his arm around saying "Help yourself," then went out and locked the door on the outside. Perhaps they did think us Russian spies after all! For the first time since leaving home I was alone. I could hardly keep from collapsing on to the double deep-mattressed bed. There were shelves of books. Of all things, they were science fiction! I felt some relief when I noticed that the one beside the bed was *Harry, the Rat with Women.*

I peeled off my clothes, revelling in being completely alone, and opened the bathroom door. Rows of bottles for purifying, smoothing and protecting the soft American male skin totalled more than I had ever used in my life. An electric toothbrush, too. I was fascinated. It moved in all directions, up and down and across, but the bristles were as soft as a baby's hair. What the bathroom did not have was a bath, I cursed the Americans again.

"I suppose a shower is better than a bath when one is utterly filthy," I thought as I tried to regulate the heat. I let the water cascade over me, till I felt like a desert after a shower of rain. I enveloped myself in the crisp clean towel and dabbed on bits of this and that from the selection of bottles. "Lanolin from genuine sheep," read one bottle, "Genuine olive oil from our hygienic laboratories," read another. I collapsed on the bed, between two pale blue nylon sheets. I lay in heaven and slipped off to sleep.

I woke up half an hour later stifled with heat and lack of air. I gasped like a fish out of water as I stumbled to the window. It didn't open. Nor would the door. I was relieved when the phone rang and the polite voice of the "Redition" said "We are waiting for you in the bar."

My clothes felt horrid, and I wished now that I had never taken them off! I winced as I pulled my manky vest over my

head and the fine wool of my shirt felt coarse and slithery. The
boys had been in the room next door and I found them surrounded with presents—shampoo, beer cans, chewing gum.

"Have some," said Roger, handing me a packet. I took three
chews and then my teeth crunched on a piece of metal. I spat
it out into my hand. A large stopping—from my back tooth!
"Troubles always start when you reach civilisation," I thought,
as twinges of toothache began to shiver in my jaw.

We were escorted down to the bar. It was civilised and plastic,
completely incongruous in its situation. No nude pictures, or
any of the raw maleness one meets in mining camps or forestry
and military isolated posts. The men were clean and shaved,
with the face beautifiers dutifully employed.

I was passed a tumbler of brandy—"Real French," said a
big-handed, open-faced man. He told me he had eleven
children and a farm. "We'd a bad harvest last year, so I came
out to earn a spot of cash." This meant £200 a week, to drive
the yellow tractor. Most men earned more, and it was the
money that brought them here, not the adventure of working
in this fabulous land of ice and snow. Not for them the magic
of the Northern Lights. There were fifty-four men here now, to
raise the building on jacks above the snow. The usual comple-
ment was twenty-five. There was no social level of class, but a
far more snobbish segregation lay in how far into the building
one was allowed. A tractor driver, for instance, only on this
floor, a wireless technician one higher up, but only a small
handful on to the top storey, and only two into the nerve
centre itself. A few Danes were on the staff—cooks and cleaners,
a Danish Government proviso that went with allowing the
Americans the use of these "Defence Areas" in Greenland.

My farmer friend kept clicking his "instantaneous" Polaroid
camera, then asking me to sign the pale dead-looking results.
"Say, what are you getting paid for this stunt of yours?" asked
my farmer's buddy. He obviously didn't believe my answer
that we weren't. How could I explain that it would take years
of writing and lecturing to pay off the cost, if ever!

"Hey," the owner of my bed and electric toothbrush interrupted, "how about phoning the folks back home? There is no one on the Hot Line to Europe just now."

I couldn't think of a number. The Americans obviously thought me daft as I struggled with my mental blank, but I'd buried such information well down in my mind. Who expects to be asked a phone number in the middle of nowhere? One came to my head. Was it my mother's or the butcher's?

I held the end of an ordinary-looking phone, while my "Redition" spoke to the base at Søndre Strømfjord, then Iceland, the Faroes, Fylingdales, each remote voice bending the American words to suit their intonation. Then the unmistakable, uncontaminated-by-any-American, Morningside, accents of the Edinburgh Exchange.

"Hullo, hullo—what's the matter?" The phone shook in my hand. It was my mother, her high-pitched voice resonant in the ridiculous cocktail bar. I couldn't speak. I handed the phone to Hugh. What can one say? "How are you?" "Fine thanks." "It's 2 a.m., you know," said my mother, and of course it was! Suddenly I overflowed with words but it was too late. There is nothing as dead as a hung-up phone.

Suddenly I felt claustrophobic in this metal box. I looked for the boys, Roger had sunk towards the plastic counter, a glassy look in his eye, and Bill was deep in conversation with the only Dane on the premises, who spoke only two words of English. They both jerked to life when Hugh suggested we should go. The men about us bustled about, changing films and attaching yet more cameras about their necks. A man in a chef's hat pushed through the crowd and asked me to sign his notebook. I looked in his eye and suddenly felt a wave of affinity with this Danish cook. We spoke a different language but we were both here for the same reasons. He understood the polar world and didn't have to ask what on earth was the point of our journey. He also knew just how great a journey it was. The Americans had no idea, but we couldn't blame them. They had flown here straight from the aerodrome in the States—a four-and-a-half-hour journey from one centrally heated establishment to another; and they would get for it a sum of money. The Danes would get a fraction of the money, but an extra width to their minds.

Hugh looked around for the "boss" to say goodbye. We found him eating cornflakes in the canteen. Everyone else dressed up to see us off. Our wind-proofs were on in a jiffy, but we had to wait for the big Americans to don their layers of insulating garments to keep them safe from the horrors of the "great outside". I was desperate to get out of the artificial air, but then frightened of the sixty-foot ladder to reach the ground. The American faces blinked in the sunlight and huddled into their coats as we all walked over to our sledge. We harnessed up, trying to look efficient. I stood on my bootlace and fell flat on my face and Roger twisted his trace with Bill's and had to untie the knot. Cameras clicked from all directions. The Danish cook came up to shake hands and I felt genuine warmth and concern and admiration in his clasp. To the Americans we were only a rather mad diversion, or a "stunt" as the farmer had said.

The sun was sinking behind a belt of clouds. There was a golden light on the snow, a radiance in the air. I was alive again. The wind was behind us, the going downhill. We set off at a cracking pace, the sledge snaking along behind. The air was crisp and invigorating on my face. An enormous distance swept before us, inviting us to come and mark its surface with our tracks. I pushed my sticks into the snow, propelling myself forward faster and faster. I felt elated with the realisation that we were part of the view—one could live in it and travel through it. I felt the pleasure that one surprisingly gets from doing something that is difficult.

We travelled ten miles at our fastest speed, and then I remembered the presents. There had been some cardboard boxes tied on to the sledge when we came out of Dye 2. What was in them? I cannot resist parcels, and I could not wait now. The boys pitched the tent while I fussed over the packages, prodding them and trying to guess, and trying to suppress the feeling at the back of my mind that I was going to be disappointed.

"Hope it's bread," said Roger longingly as at last we all crowded into the tent. I tore the longest box open. Oranges! Dozens of them! "Have to eat them all tonight," said Hugh. "We can't possibly pull them on the sledge. They weigh a ton." I was into the next box while Roger and Bill attacked an orange each. It was full of little packets—"Irresistibly, Instant Tea". Another box still, but I hardly dared to open it. Surely it would have bread? No, twenty-four bars of "Almond Candy" and my tooth ached even more at the thought.

We were tired out—apart from the stress of our eight hours of social life, we had travelled for two nights and a day with nothing but a cat-nap to keep us going. I slithered into my sleeping-bag, with a large orange in each hand, but I was too tired to take off the skin. I looked at the luscious round balls, and the difficulty of reaching the flesh seemed insurmountable. I fell asleep with them still clutched in my hands.

We slept all day long. I stirred now and then to the sound of someone sucking an orange. The hours slipped by . . . I woke up properly with a warm sticky feeling round my hips. I had lain on an orange. There was a rustle of sweetie paper and I found that the boys were demolishing the candy bars. "There's your pile," indicated Hugh with his elbow, his mouth too full of glutinous toffee. "You can't resist Instant Tea," said Roger solemnly handing me a cup of hot water and a packet of powder. Orange skins surrounded us, and pips were everywhere. I felt marvellously over-indulged and I could see that the boys were relishing it too. "I love to be weak," said Hugh, ripping open another candy bar and sinking back into his sleeping-bag for another stretch of sleep. Suddenly he sat up, a look of horror on his face. "I've left my long johns and vest in the chief's bed." "Hugh," I gasped in horror, "they were absolutely revolting. What ever will he think?" "It'll put him off his cornflakes," said Roger, trying not to laugh.

VI

Nansen had erected a sail on his sledge and we had hoped to do the same. His efforts were so successful that at one point his sledge tore off without him. It scarcely seemed to touch the snow as it whirled over the rough surface, jumping from crest to crest of the drifts, leaving him lying flat out in the snow, watching it fade into the distance, feeling rather foolish at being left behind. He struggled to his feet and set off in pursuit. The snow was littered with precious belongings that had fallen off. These could not be abandoned and so he loaded himself up, clutching boxes of provisions under each arm, a fur jacket slung round his neck, an ice axe through his belt. When he discovered the box of special meat chocolate, there was nothing to be done but sit down and wait for the others to discover that he had fallen off the sledge. and come back to look. But his companion Sverdrup, steering the sledge from the front, was quite oblivious that Nansen was not sitting comfortably on behind. He sailed along merrily and even chatted over his shoulder. He did wonder why there was no response, but could not see round the sledge. A little farther on he tried again to talk, then called louder. He began to shout at the top of his voice, but still there was no reply. The sailing was so exciting that he went on farther still before turning the sledge to the wind and going round to see what was the matter. He found his passenger gone. It was very difficult for Sverdrup to lower the sail by himself, but at last he did and waited hopefully for Nansen to turn up. They waited for each other till both were driven to move by the piercing icy wind.

They now lashed all their sledges together into one big boat, with trailing ropes for the "crew" to hold on. Nansen did some steering from the front, and describes it as "exciting work". To me, his descriptions sounds pretty desperate. The steerer must not fall, or he would be mown down by the sledge and ground into the snow. He had to keep his skis firmly together, and ride over the waves of snow, or through the soft drifts. They had only one "ski pole", so balancing was precarious, yet they flew along at breakneck pace, shouting to each other and laughing with the thrill of speed. Nansen's was a happy expedition, even when things were very much against them, as they often were. His party were good friends to start with, and even firmer friends at the end: very different from most of the sagas of polar travel, where the officers issued orders to the men.

The wind was now refreshing, spilling over the summit of the Inland Ice, and beating on the back of our tent. Roger had been waiting for this. He burrowed in the bottom of the "sledge gear" bag and unearthed a large orange sail. He had given a lot of thought to the stepping of a mast and we had been carrying two bamboo poles at the bottom of the sledge for this purpose. Roger now completely stripped the sledge—there was only one pole! I looked back hopefully at our tracks. Had it fallen off one mile back or 253?

"Never mind", said Roger, as unperturbed as ever. "I'll just make one with your ski sticks." "Mine!" I bristled with indignation. Of course, I didn't pull as hard as the boys and they never once suggested that I should. "But, but . . ." "All right, all right," said Hugh hastily, "use mine."

Bill and I packed up the tent. The biggest job was burying the orange peel! There were still a few oranges left and we shoved them away in the camera bag. Then we stood around stamping our feet, as Hugh and Roger fought with pieces of nylon string. They looked about ready and I started to load on the bags. "No good," said Hugh. "We'll have to try it the other way round." Bill and I looked at each other with irritation. It all seemed such a waste of time. We were going fine without the silly sail, why bother about it at all?

But they tried again and then standing at either side of the sledge, they pulled on the vital ends of the pink nylon string, and the sail unfurled. The wind charged into it, billowing it out, and, miraculously, the sledge started to move. Hastily we harnessed up and rushed to the front and skied off. Like a ghostly galleon, the sledge rumbled along on our heels, threatening to bowl us over at any minute. Roger and Hugh felt it more than Bill and I, and they kept getting mixed up in my trace as they overtook me. "I can't go any faster," I shouted at Hugh, exasperated by him tripping me up for the fifth time. "Go at the back then, as an anchor," he roared, the wind catching his words. I clipped on my rope to the rear of the sledge and we set off again. "Irresistibly Instant," I thought as the animated sledge took off before the boys started to pull on their trace. They had to hurry to keep in front.

My view now was of the billowing orange sail. When I could not keep up, I stood on my skis and let the sledge draw me along.

Marvellous! I felt weightless and the sensation was like a dream. I was floating, my skis carrying me on irresistibly across the silky surface of this magnificent gleaming world, separated from the sky only by a thin line of the white horizon.

"What's the mileage?" roared Hugh and I stumbled back to normal life. "Three," I replied, reading off the scale. "That's four miles per hour," shouted Hugh triumphantly and the hours ticked by once more. I was reluctant to stop at 1 a.m. "Been going six hours," said Hugh, but I could not believe that we had. Onion soup and instant tea, then off once more. In no time at all it was 7 a.m. and the boys came exhaustedly to a stop.

"What's up?" I said accusingly, feeling absolutely fresh. But they were dead beat, having put their all into keeping in front of the sledge. I didn't like to admit that I had been a passenger all the way.

"Two hundred miles in ten days," said Hugh with satisfaction, leaning over Roger's shoulder as he plotted out his chart. "See land soon." I was electrified by the thought. Was there an end, after all, to this white saucer of which we never reached the rim? Bill interrupted my thoughts by rushing past me, muttering "Too many oranges," and I remembered my aching tooth—all that we had left from our visit to Chicken Maryland!

"Meat-bar stew—whoa," shouted Hugh, with an animated noise, and even I looked forward to it too, after two days of oranges and almond bar. The successful day had put our minds on a higher plane than usual and we talked as we spooned up our stew. Roger told us stories of the old days of sail, his beard and side-whiskers making him a figure from his tales. Hugh's beard somehow looked perpetually mangy and had a habit of trapping a fair proportion of his porridge in its long red swirls. Bill's made him the cartoon Highlander, a William Wallace straight from the heather and ready for the fray. I was too tired to talk for long. I understood now why peasants so seldom get out of the rut. One is just too tired after a day of physical effort to read or even think. I dipped my buttered biscuit into the sugar, face down: the height of indulgence in our limited life.

The days slipped by, at twenty-five miles a time. Glorious days of billowing sail, creaking snow and snaking sledge bounding restlessly on. The air was crisp, like the best January day at home, yet here it was summer, July 16th. We were losing altitude fast, and several times I saw land, only for it to float away as a bank of cloud—luckily before I had told the others of these manifestations! But—there was something ahead. A dark line across the snow.

As we drew nearer, the line opened up and turned out to be a lake. "Trouble," pronounced Hugh and he was only too right. We had reached the level of the summer thaw. Water from the melting snow collected on the surface, forming areas of bog and marsh, unable to drain properly as the angle was not steep enough for the water to run away down hill nor could it sink into the lower layers of solid ice. In polar circles, this is called "morass".

Reluctantly we lowered the sail. We would have to change course, and go round the rim of the lake lying across our path. I folded up the beautiful orange sail and stuffed it away in the bag. It had certainly earned its keep.

We skirted the blue water glinting in the sun, but there was another lake in front. I recognised the dark line that opened up, shining blue, as we drew near. We zigzagged to and fro, then all stopped, transfixed by a roaring noise. It was running water, extraordinary to my ears after the silence of the Inland Ice. A stream was flowing from lake to lake, charging at a great speed, having no friction of stones or rock to hold it back. Gingerly we approached its bank, then carefully placed our skis across as a bridge. One heave on our sticks and we were over, ready to haul on the sledge. "That was easy," I thought. Suddenly my skis broke the surface and I felt the chill of icy water creeping up my legs. I tried to hurry on, but my weight smashed through again and again. Memories of the sea ice! There were ripples on the open water on my left; I felt excited at the life of movement in spite of my frozen feet. I moved my toes, hoping to warm up the water sloshing about in my boots. I had to get used to having something to look at, something ahead to reach, something to measure the distance with and watch it go by.

Hugh brought us to a stop. Perhaps the surface would freeze if we waited till the middle of the night. I took off my skis and then sank up to my thigh in soft wet slush! How could we camp? We were all floundering about, dragging a leg out of the morass only for the other foot to sink in even deeper. Hugh had an idea, and we watched sceptically while he carefully laid the skis in a row, then set about pitching the tent on top.

"Oh look what you've done," he said to me in his most hurt voice. I had stood in the area to be covered by the tent and the hole I had made was filling up with water, till it lapped over the top. "Wash basin laid on," I explained, but he didn't think it funny.

We lay full length in the tent, to extend our weight over as big an area as possible. I leant on my elbow, and it sank into the surface like a knife in processed cheese. Roger lay on his front, plotting and replotting our position. We must come off the ice at one particular point, or else we would be tied up in impassable rivers and uncrossable arms of fjords. The point that Hugh had decided would give us the easiest route off was marked "Point 660" on the map. Two miles off course in either direction and we could miss it. Hugh fiddled with the wireless. The aerodrome at Søndre Strømfjord was supposed to send out a constant signal to be picked up by homing planes, like a lighthouse on our coasts. He hoped to be able to pick it up on our little set, but from what distance we didn't know.

If I lay absolutely still I was quite comfortable, but one move and a ski binding bit into my hip. I turned my head, and water bubbled into the depression under the ground sheet. I became aware of a ghastly smell, and pinned it down to Hugh's wet socks, lying an inch from my head. He was most indignant when I suggested he move them! Roger's sextant was lying near my hand, and I picked it up and twisted the mirror until I could squint at a part of my face. It was quite extraordinary! There were white blotches of unpigmented skin on either cheek, like leprosy, and my nose shone scarlet between scales of dark brown. Heavens, it would have to clear up quickly, before we reached Søndre Strømfjord. I looked across the tent. "How far, Roger?" Could we trust his navigation? His arithmetic was hopeless, worse even than mine, and I had my doubts, but Hugh and Bill never breathed a word of lack of confidence. Now he was redoing his calculations and they came out to a different result.

"Well," said Hugh, "it's been a crumpet trip this, we're due for some difficulties." He was absolutely sure that, whatever they were, they would not be too much for us to overcome.

The snow seemed firmer when Bill stirred us up at 1 a.m. An enormous moon hung low in the sky on our left, the kind one sees only in books of nursery rhymes, with the cow poised ready to jump. It was a silvery yellow and I felt I could nearly prod it if I jumped up with a ski stick in my hand. The sun was creeping up fast on our right, and by 4 a.m. both balls were in the sky. Great shafts of light shone down, and a play of shadow came and went across the ice.

We were going towards an obvious area of morass, lying

completely across our path. As we drew nearer we could hear a
river running through the middle. Should we detour round it?
It might stretch for miles. "Oh let's go through," said Bill,
ski-ing confidently towards the roaring torrent. "The area
must be well drained with that burn in spate." No one argued.

As we approached the banks, the sledge started to sink. The
boys went back to give it a heave. I was in front. Suddenly I
was up to my waist in freezing water. I couldn't move. My
skis were trapped. A strong current was sweeping them side-
ways. I couldn't get my hand down to release them. The more I
floundered the more the ice broke about me. I fell on my side
and was now up to my neck. I felt desperate. Where were the
boys? I was still attached to the sledge and Roger was now
hauling on my trace. Bill was struggling to keep the sledge
upright and Hugh was taking photos! At last I could grab
Roger's leg and he landed me, sodden and shivering, my
breath gasping out with the cold. We retraced our steps—my
only thought was to get the tent up, primus on, and me in my
dry sleeping-bag. We floundered through into the morass
again and again, the boys heaving and thrutching on the sledge,
me fumbling on behind, holding grimly on to the rope that
joined me to the only solid thing on the landscape. At last
we reached a patch of drier snow, slightly higher than its
surroundings. Water spurted out of the holes in my mukluks
like fountains every time I put down my feet, but the fleeting
pleasure of standing on "dry" ground compensated for the
discomfort of the moment. I could feel the sun boring through
my anorak but I knew it couldn't warm my frozen core.

Hugh and Bill immediately set off on a reconnaissance. We
had to get over the river somehow. The thought of a detour
made me feel quite sick. Roger and I gingerly pitched the tent,
treading like cats, frightened that we might break the precious
surface. When at last I could go in, I didn't want to and pottered
about outside in the sun. Would we ever get out of this maze?
Looking around from where we were, it seemed hopeless; lakes
in all directions and that frantic river tearing along its bed of

polished ice, cutting off our access to the west. I felt despair creeping up my legs. The main difference between the men and me was not their physical brawn but their resources of mental strength. I would be very surprised if a team of women alone could cross the Greenland ice; I think their ability to keep slogging on would be flooded by emotion, which would lose them the day. If a Russian team of females does prove me wrong, I shall query their hormones.

The others came back. Their bright enthusiastic faces made me think that they had found a way, forgetting that they did not think a hurdle a disaster. "An excellent salmon torrent," shouted Hugh when in earshot, "but we can't possibly get across." I was for going back up the river, Roger and Bill for following it down. "Sleep on it," said Hugh, tired out, and we all agreed.

*　　　*　　　*

We decided to go back. The sun was setting as we loaded up, like a vast furnace just behind the clouds, throwing fire up into the enormous sky; yellows and russets and vivid streaks of red. It was fantastic—the backcloth for a desperate battle of life and death. Bill burst into song—"Kishmull's Galley"—the strange, off beat Gaelic melody an addition to the desperate scarlet and black sky.

We retraced our tracks, then worked our way round a basin at the head of our river system. The surface was peculiarly glazed and we sped along over the top. Like so many dreaded things, it wasn't really as bad as I had expected. We crossed one river easily, then another, over the top of a lake, and now we could head west again. I was congratulating us on the speedy return to the proper direction when we suddenly came up to a major torrent, so deep in its banks that there was very little sound to warn us of its presence. We veered left again, and came to the lake that gave the river its head. Round it we went. Another river—wide and sluggish like stretches of the Tay.

"Hell's teeth," I thought, "we could follow this for days and be no better off." The same thought had hit the boys. "Nothing for it," said Hugh, taking off his skis. He then sat down and slipped his crampons on to his boots. He attached the end of a length of rope round his waist and handed the coils to Bill. Then he slithered down the bank and I held my breath as the water crept up to his ankles, knees, thighs, waist. He braced himself against the current and slipped one foot slowly nearer the opposite bank, then the other, fighting for his balance against the buffeting of the current. I breathed again as his hips started to appear, then his legs and then he at last heaved himself out on the far side. He yelled instructions to us, but of course we couldn't hear. Luckily Roger had the same ideas, and we spread out the ground sheet on the emptied sledge, then wrapped up the first load. We attached another rope to our end, then launched our "boat". Bill slithered down beside it, placing the claws of his crampons carefully so that they bit into the river bed. The current caught the sledge, swinging it round, rocking it, throwing up waves all round it. Bill and Hugh hauled and hauled on the rope, but the current was too much for them. The sledge was pulling them rather than they it. Hugh was coming nearer and nearer to the brim of the bank. Roger and I could do nothing but watch. Bill had now reached the far bank. He clambered up, swung the rope over his shoulder, and braced himself for another try. I could see him straining, his face twisted with concentration and effort, and he was pulling the rope in, inch by inch. The sledge, like an angry bull at the end of a tether, was being pulled in. Hugh leapt back into the water to heave it up the bank and in a few minutes it was our turn to pull in the rope. Empty, I found the sledge a dead weight, how had they handled it full? The rope slipped through my gloves, so I shook them off. I will never make that mistake again! The wet rope was freezing as it came out of the water, and it cut into my hands as if they were jelly, solidifying my fingers into a clenched position. I abandoned the job to Roger and desperately tried to pull my gloves back on to my hands, but now they were wet too and freezing fast and I could get my hands only into the palm. The fingers flapped, stiff and useless.

As the sledge was ferried across, five times, I remembered with a sickening jolt that I had never altered my size 4 crampons to suit my size 7 mukluked feet. I remembered exactly the time I had intended doing the job in Billy's garden when we were packing up, but the sun had come out and I had lain flat out with my head in my arms, too lazy to stir. I looked now at my useless crampons lying beside Roger's in the snow. I would have to cross without them. "You carry the cameras," said Roger, it never occurring to him that I would fall. "I'll bring the sextant and my sleeping-bag." I slipped the karabiner, a metal snap link, at my waist on to the rope that sloshed across the river and edged one foot into the water. It was agonisingly cold for an instant, then I forgot about it as I felt my way across, shuffling my toes forward slowly, inch by inch, resisting the batter of the current about my thighs. It got deeper. I had a mental battle now, not to just let go and let the current sweep me away. It was the easiest thing to do. But one's common sense, or guardian angel, never lets one give in. I had to push my legs against the water, force a way through against its resistance. It became shallower. I looked up. Bill's face was just above me. He was hauling in my rope, not trusting me an inch. Hugh grabbed the camera—his one worry—and I clambered up the bank.

Roger joined us unperturbed and Hugh stood on the sledge to take a photo. Someone moved, nudged the sledge, and it started to slither back down the bank. Hugh lost his balance. His arms flayed, his body arched—and he just managed to jump on to the bank. It broke under his weight and he ended up at the water's edge, upright, but only just.

Bill, Roger and I laughed and laughed. I collapsed on the snow doubled up; even Hugh thought it funny, but we found it hilarious. "Come on," chivvied Bill as last, and eventually we set off again, with water dripping out of the sodden sleeping-bags leaving a dirty trail in the snow. Clods of snow stuck on to our wet skis, till the weight seemed as if it would break my ankle in two. Suddenly we became aware of another river on our right, running across our tracks, but to the south—the one we had just crossed ran north.

"Oh, Hell, let's camp," I advocated in despair. "We've done nine miles anyway," said Roger, "even if they were mostly backwards." Four weeks ago to this day we left the boat. In two weeks' time the children would arrive. We had only about fifty miles between us and the edge of the ice-cap, but on today's progress we wouldn't get off within months. My musings were interrupted by a tearing noise. I looked round to see Roger standing crestfallen with the legs of his pyjama bottoms in his hand. He wore them instead of long johns. "They were brand new," he said indignantly, a leg in either hand. "I only gave them a pull, and they just came apart." He was far more put out by this than any difficulty we encountered on the trip. Should I offer to sew them back on? They hadn't been washed or even taken off since we started. Roger's smile got the better of me and I dug out my needle and thread.

* * *

When I've done my work of day
And I row my boat away
Down the waters of Loch Tay
When the evening light is fading
And I gaze upon Ben Lawers
Where the after glory glows
And I dream of two bright eyes
And a merry mouth below
Hi-re, Hi-re, Hi-ro.

Bill roared out the Tay Boat Song as he stirred the porridge. We set off at 10 p.m. into another golden night. The going was surprisingly easy and we covered the ground quickly, up to the top of a new water system running off to our left. The morasses seemed to have dried out, so we crunched over thousands of little pinnacles of ice. Suddenly I froze in my tracks. Land! Or was it? I moved on again, willing myself not to look again for another ten minutes. It *was* land! A mountain with a snow on top. I looked back at the others. Roger had seen it too, and not said anything in case it drifted away. Our goal was at last in sight. Like homing dogs, we cracked up the pace, our skis rattling over the dry surface. I could not take my eyes off the horizon. The mountain remained solid and firm. Dry land. A lake of beautiful agate blue appeared, and we had a second breakfast by its side. My feet were dry! I could hardly believe it after the last days of constant bog. We had covered seventeen miles already on this haul and were raring for more.

Our next stop was at a crevasse. I was thrilled to see it. It meant that we were now really on the edge of the ice-cap, where the glaciers bend off to meet the sea. I have always hated crevasses before, always expecting to be swallowed up in their yawning gaps, but now I was pleased. Another great jagged rip across our path and the moment had come to take off our skis. My feet felt peculiar and light but it was miraculous to stand on the surface instead of sinking up to my knees. I couldn't help gazing towards the land. I could now see valleys and hills, and the sun glinting on patches of water. Point 660 without a doubt. As we strode towards it, more land appeared on either side, more hills and valleys and lakes. Slowly it began to dawn on us all that the stretch of land of about fifty miles' breadth was identical. Which point in fact, was 660?

Roger got out his sextant, his graph, the map, the aerial photos, and Hugh fiddled with the wireless. Suddenly a strong signal burst out, da de, da da—da de da da. Hugh swung the arm on top till the rangefinder showed maximum intensity. It pointed well to our left. Da de da da—it rang out mysteriously from the little black box. We clustered round, fascinated. "Søndre Strømfjord for sure," said Hugh, "and in that case, that's not Point 660." We were still higher than the hills in front of us, and now that we had shortened the distance between us, our mecca did not look as beckoning as before. "Press on," was the verdict after an hour of argument to and fro. The distance looked only about fifteen miles, and another day's march would get us near enough to see where we really were.

The ice was now under pressure, held back by the range of hills, so it was forced up into a surface that looked like the moon. Dunes of ice were pushed up, some hillocks with sheer ice walls and narrow crests, some hummocks the size of a house. The entire surface was heaved up into this rugged formation, which got worse and more hectic as we approached the edge of the ice-cap and came on to the glaciers that flowed down to meet the sea. We toiled away, each hummock had to be scrambled up, the sledge hauled till it pivoted on the top, then held back as it thundered down the other side, threatening to crash to smithereens on the wall of the hummock in front. I began to hate the sledge as I heaved and pushed from behind, then clung on as it dragged me off my feet on the far side. It bashed my legs and tore at my hands. I cricked my back pushing and ricked my neck holding it from running away. And still the land looked no nearer. We camped, exhausted, having covered fifteen miles in the day, but ten in the wrong direction. I couldn't stay inside the tent and crouched outside, gazing towards the land. I belonged there, not to this ice and snow and frozen sea. I was watching when the morning light crept over the hills, then shone on some water in the distance. Søndre Strømfjord for sure.

*   *   *

Our mukluks were on their last legs, and we were all counting the cost. Roger's feet had rubbed right through a piece of elastoplast over a blister, and his socks were a gory red. We pottered about, sewing them up, mending a cracked spar on the sledge, threading a cord round an anorak waist. There seemed to be a holiday feeling among us, a feeling that there was "heaps of time", and also a strong reluctance to arrive. I felt I wanted to hold on to our isolation for as long as possible.

Bill, as usual, urged us on; another day of fighting the hummocks, forcing a way through the great ridges and steep gulleys between. A whole day and we were no closer. "All right then," said Hugh. "Two people press on, on foot, and jolly well reach that land. Carry a load and don't come back without getting off the ice."

Roger and Hugh were the best at handling the sledge. They nursed it over the ridges of ice, and gently lowered it down, again and again, never in despair The worse the situation, the better Hugh and Roger worked together, and it never occurred to them that they would fail. So it was to be Bill and I that set off to find the land.

We chose a lightish load, roped up together, and said goodbye. What was difficult sledging country made ideal walking, and we sped over the ice, jumping from hummock to hummock, crossing the odd crevasse by a convenient narrow bridge of snow. The others soon dropped out of sight. We stopped every now and then to stick a ski stick in to guide us back, to show us the way through the maze of hummocks and hillocks of ice.

Up over a hummock, particularly steep, and another and another. The ice was thrown up into a fantastic hotch-potch of crevasses and canyons. Up another crest and my eye was caught by black rocks. There was land below me. I screamed at Bill and he ran to my side to see whatever was the matter.

A wave of excitement carried us down a slithery ridge of bare ice, and we were off. We scrambled over the rubble of the edge of a moraine, pushed in front by the ever-moving ice, and we were there. Music! It was a snow bunting, bustling about among the stones, trilling his joy of the morning. Purple saxifrage and tufts of moss campion grew among the boulders at the edge of the moraine. Tears splashed down my face as I bent to pick them in my hands. A little farther still to go, then green grass. I threw myself down and buried my face and hands in the real, solid land. The smell of it and feel of it made me choke with excitement and emotion. Something moving caught my eye. A reindeer! It lifted its head, with its over-weight antlers, and looked me in the eye, then went back to graze.

"I feel like a child with a new toy," said Bill between a smile that split his face. I remembered this remark, as it was unlike Bill to talk of his emotions. But this was great enough to overcome any inhibitions. We were at the bottom of a little hill—was it Point 660? I pulled myself together and followed Bill as he scambled up to the top. Then we sat down in a little niche between some red warm rocks, and Bill produced some chocolate. I unwrapped it, by feel, not daring to take my eyes off the view in case it was all a dream. Below us was a meadow, with reindeer grazing peacefully, undisturbed. Then rolling hills, and in the distance the gleam of water—Søndre Strømfjord. Bill spread out the map and we matched it to the scene. "Well I'm convinced," said Bill, and so was I. Slightly above the reindeer pasture was a little lake of purest blue. "Let's camp there tomorrow night." "O.K.," said Bill and we forced ourselves to get up, to tear away from the delightful land and pitch ourselves against the ice once more. It was the most difficult thing I have ever done in my life, to have to go back to the deadly world of ice and snow, and leave all this behind.

I picked some flowers for Hugh as we ran back down the hill, and some stones from the moraine, and then we forced ourselves back on to the ice. "Perhaps they are nearly here," I thought hopefully, as we recrossed ridge after ridge, back through the maze of hummocks, forcing ourselves on, uphill. But no sign. No life. No movement on the ice. "We're practically back where we started from," said Bill indignantly, when I noticed the sun glinting on something on the ice. It was a tin. I ran to it, then suddenly saw that there were hundreds of tins, scattered and smashed and squashed. We heard voices and climbed another hummock. I looked down on more tins, and in the midst of them sat Hugh and Roger, with a blissful smile on their faces, and a can at their lips. "Have a beer," said Roger

sweeping his arm in a generous gesture. That's what they were.
Beer cans! Bill attacked one with his axe and a spew of froth
hit him on the face. I did the same, and drank back the cold
delicious liquid. I completely forgot that I didn't like beer. I
threw the empty can over my shoulder and chose another and
another. . . .

Roger and Hugh had had enough, and were laying in a stock
on the sledge. Up until now we had been throwing anything
away to lighten it—now it reached its heaviest yet. Where
had all the beer come from? Our speculations became more
and more bizarre.

Only when we were snug in the tent, pitched surprisingly
squint, did I remember to give Hugh his presents. He turned
the pebbles over in his hand, feeling, as I had, the life and
vitality of the green land. I could not describe it to him. It
meant so much to me that I was inarticulate, frightened of
spoiling it with too many words.

The next day we were all off the ice. We carried the sledge
over the boulders and put it gently down on the grass. I watched
Hugh and Roger. Their reaction was the same as mine. They
threw themselves on to the ground, feeling it, relishing it, then
scrambled up the little hillock that was all that Point 660
turned out to be and sat on the earth, their backs against the
warm solid boulders, gazing over the rolling hills to the west. I
went for a walk. For the first time there was somewhere to
walk to, something to get behind, something to see. My eyes
darted over the ground. I had such a thrill from a new flower,
a beetle. Then my biggest excitement yet. A big white boulder
moved: a fat Arctic hare. Its black-tipped ears twitched and it
looked me full in the face, its nose wrinkling in curiosity. I sat
down and watched it eating grass. Only when it had had
enough did it turn round, kick up its back feet and scamper
away. Suddenly I started to cry. Reaction, bottled-up emotion
—just the relaxation of being alone and able to cry if I felt like
it. Hugh found me, and I buried my head on his shoulder. I
didn't have to explain what I was crying about—he was crying too.

That evening we pitched the tent beside the bright blue lake. Tufts of white cotton grass bobbed on long stalks in at the waters edge, disturbed by the movement of two brown ducks. The grass of green, with splatters of yellow and pink. We didn't use the groundsheet or the kampamats. We didn't want anything to come between us and the ground. A mother reindeer came down to drink, a soft little calf at her side.

The lake was cradled in green, and you had to look up, above the rise, to see the startling white of the Inland Ice. I could look at it dispassionately now, without feeling the pain in frozen fingers or the agony of snow crystals hurled in one's face. Four hundred miles of it lay behind us. In front was thirty miles of land, but no difficulty could stop us now. I loved the feeling of my bare feet on the soft grass as I wandered to the water's edge. I pulled off my clothes, and launched myself in. For an instant the cold caught at my breath. Then it was marvellous. The water embraced me, lapping off the sweat and grime of so much effort. I swam lazily until the cold drove me out. Then with a magnificent gesture I threw in my clothes. Just at that instant a breeze got up, whipped over the water, and my bra and long johns sailed out of reach. I shouted to Roger, and gallant as ever, he threw himself in to retrieve them, swimming with long lazy strokes. I felt eyes watching me; it was reindeer, lots of them, strolling down to have a look at these peculiar creatures who had turned up on their favourite pasture where they always came to drink.

Bill had soup ready when I got back. It was lovely in the tent, leaning on the soft tundra cushions of moss and grass. I felt a great affection for my companions in the tent, each of whom had been vital in the journey—Bill's strength, Roger's navigation. I looked at Hugh, trimming his beard with Roger's penknife, and knew he felt the same. It had never occurred to either of us that anyone would let us down. We just knew that we would all give of our best and that that would be enough to get us through. I felt like Augustin Courtauld, who said that he hated reaching a journey's end. After his fantastic seven hundred-mile journey with Gino Watkins in an open boat down the south-west coast of Greenland, when there was no room to carry food, he said that he was overcome with the futility of their endeavour and the smallness of their achievement. I know exactly what he meant. Suddenly the companionship that comes with sharing a life of uncertainty, danger and disappointment, joy and success, is shattered. One's relationship with people in normal life never reaches this closeness, this awareness of each other's feelings and thoughts. It is a precious thing, and I hate to let it go.

The same names crop up again and again in the stories of expeditions to the North, as if one has to come back and see it all again. One forgets the near misses and the cold and remembers only the bright sun, clear air and the companions who shared it all too.

Nansen returned in his unique ship the *Fram*, built with a rounded hull that would enable her to rise up above the ice when squeezed by a closing pack. He took her towards the Pole, then let her drift with the winter's ice till it seemed unlikely that she would go closer, at which point Nansen set off on foot. He had to turn back with two hundred and forty miles still to go, missed the boat still drifting in the pack, and spent five months of incredible journeying before reaching the Franz Josef islands off Spitzbergen. His great companion Sverdrup eventually turned up with the *Fram*.

After this, Nansen devoted his enthusiasm to politics. He must have felt that something must be done to improve the world, quickly, after the horrors of the World War. It was no use waiting for others to do it; he would have to get involved himself. So he suppressed his own longing for the desolation, yet tranquillity, of the polar world, to fight other people's battles.

He became a principal pillar of the League of Nations, right from its start. When he came up against red tape in trying to organise an international loan to provide famine relief in 1921, after the Russian Revolution, he went ahead himself and raised £250,000 from the public in six weeks. And in those days a £1 was a £1. He by-passed officialdom, organised a small staff of administrators, plus Mr. Hoover of America, and fed ten million starving people. He then became a champion of human rights and fought for the settlement of refugees: tens of thousands of white Russians with nowhere to go, masses of Greeks from Asia Minor, thousands of people uprooted by a world war. Nansen instigated the idea of a passport for these "stateless" people, and he forced his scheme through endless sessions of the League of Nations, until practically every government had accepted it. For 450,000 stateless people, without a recognised nationality, this became known as a "Nansen Passport", and the European world showed its appreciation of his efforts by awarding him the Nobel Peace Prize in 1922. Britain seems to have paid little attention to this great man with the cares of the world in his heart and the energy to do something about it. St. Andrews University did what it could—the students made him Rector in 1926.

I am sure that Nansen's philanthropy stemmed from the years he had spent in the North, where the frontiers were the vast, unreachable horizons, and the only enemy one's own lack of strength to go on. He expected a world where people helped each other as a matter of course, and where each man's voice was as important as the next.

Shackleton, Gino Watkins, Scott, they all returned eventually to bury themselves in the snow. Names like Steffansen, Rasmussen and Mylius Ericksen are ingrained in the ice of north Greenland, which they got to know so well. Ejnar Mikkelsen first tasted the magic of Greenland in an open boat journey down the east coast. He had an indomitable will and a great sense of humour, and I wish I could have been one of his companions, although I don't think I could have laughed as his men did when out of food, when forced to tear their sleeping-bags in half to cut down the weight, or when the dogs devastated the camp, eating everything, even including the whips, and then snuggled down in the men's ruined bags. Mikkelsen's journey round the coast of north-east Greenland still stands as one of the most magnificent on record. He had seven hundred and fifty miles to go with only forty-five days food for himself and his companion, one quarter of that for the dogs. He hoped to pick up the food depots left by Mylius Ericksen's tragically fated party, and he was lucky. But they had to keep crossing leads of open water and morasses up to their waists. The food became sodden, a mass of soft dough, the dried vegetables swelled to three times their size, and salt water had to be squeezed out of the tea. The two men were sodden too, their sleeping-bags as bad, but Mikkelsen's light-hearted diary never gets depressed. "We ate the mould forming in the wet food happily. After all it provided us with 'green stuff' and tasted very good!" Eventually, with all the dogs dead, they had to abandon their tent, sleeping-bags, "everything that helped make life bearable", hoping to reach a hut eighty miles away. But everything went wrong. A blizzard sprang up, hurling itself at the two weak men in a fury of wind and snow. They had to hide under rocks, and valuable days slipped by before they could move again. The sea ice that they were on was thin and swayed ominously with the waves stirred up by the storm. They had to cross the ice, which was far too thin to support them, but "drowning was infinitely better than starvation" and so they pushed on. They did reach the hut and when they saw it below them, they just sat down and gazed. "At last we sighted the place it has taken us so many months of toil to reach, the place that we have talked and dreamed of for so many days. A little house—the homely comfort of the place goes to our hearts." They only just made it, shuffling their weary frost-bitten feet, dragging themselves like old men and halting again and again to rest. It was two years before a Norwegian sealer happened to put in and rescue them. A bear ate most of Mikkelsen's diary but his account in his book of these twenty-four months is none the worse for that. They spent the time talking and talking, even though there was nothing to talk about, keeping their thoughts as far as possible in the background. "Silence means the endless anxiety of waiting."

Safely home after two hundred and ten days' voyage, Mikkelsen writes, "Strange how distant and unreal it seems. In that short time the very name of Greenland has faded into something vague and far—the title of a story, wherein are told the things that happened to two men whom we once knew."

Already, one day off the ice, I felt the same.

VII

It was noisy on the tundra, after the silence of the Inland Ice. Buntings and pippets twittered among the seeds of the little shrubs, and squawking ravens appeared to be murdering each other in their nests stuffed in the cracks of the rocks. Sea birds mewed, soaring above us, and was it an eagle that nearly hit me in the face, as startled as I was, as I clambered along a ledge of rock and rounded a corner into the sun? There was a smell of summer here in July and I kept falling behind the boys as I found yet another flower that I had to crouch beside and feel. A dramatic purple bloom with dark green leaves— Arctic willow herb, but it seemed more suited to the tropics than here. Fat wintergreen with red, cabbagy leaves, or big yellow daisy heads on woolly stalks; something new all the time, but we had to press on. I was tired, my back ached, knees and thighs were stiff and heavy, and I longed just to sit down and rest, to lie in the sun, and soak up its strength. I felt like a cat that needs the sun to put vigour in its coat. But we must get to the American base before there was any panic about a rescue party. Also, the children were due in a week. Whenever I remembered this I leapt to my feet and staggered on again, hitching my load higher on my shoulders to relieve my back. It took three loads each to ferry our gear and I was always last. Recovering the same ground nearly broke my heart as well as my back.

I could see the others, putting up the tent on the river flats. It was a great grey river, coloured by the glacier silt, but the camp site looked delightful. A figure left it, retracing its tracks back towards me. It would be Roger, with his kind heart, coming to help with my load. I was right. "Seen this?" he asked as he came up and peered into a crack in the rocks behind me. "A pippet's nest." I peeped in past his fingers holding back some grass. A battery of yellow beaks was all I could see.

Next day we were faced with crossing the river. "Do a Blondin," said Hugh enthusiastically, longing to try an aerial ropeway. Roger, being tallest, crossed on a rope first. He anchored this rope up high, then remembered that he needed two. Hugh looked at me. "Oh, all right," I said, rolling up my trouser legs. The first step was all right, and the second, but the third brought the water over my calf-high mukluk and the cold gripped me in a paralysing vice. The agony of it! The current was washing me off balance now, and the tension on the rope was pulling me down stream. I edged another foot forward, the stones below it moved, and I was off my feet, swirling down with the water. I hit a rock, found my feet, lost them again in a deep hole, clung on to another rock with my arms, and again struggled to my feet. "Nearly over," shouted Roger cheerfully from above. "God damn you," I spluttered through chattering teeth. I clambered up the bank. Hugh, on the other side, looked quite unmoved.

Roger erected his aerial ropeway and the boys ferried the gear across. I looked up to see my sleeping-bag with my personal belongings poised half way, water lapping over the top. "For heaven's sake," I shouted to Roger. "Just getting on my gloves," he answered. "What's up?"

All over at last and on to another camp. As each journey had to be done three times we could only move five miles or so in a forward direction, making twenty-five in all.

Each camp was delightful, and I was always reluctant to move on. The next day's march followed the river, the map implying that it flowed in to the main water-course at the head of Søndre Strømfjord. In that case there should be no more rivers to cross. I padded along the sandy bank, my mukluks nearly through, dallying to look at a ringed plover that pottered about at the water's edge, looking like a very proper Presbyterian minister who would not dream of wetting his feet.

With a swirl and a roaring swoosh, our river suddenly bent to the left, to avoid flowing into a lake, and disappeared into a black and sinister gorge.

My load grew heavier as I gazed crestfallen at the lake. I could not walk all the way round. The boys dumped their loads here and went back for more. I rested my back on the bank. A sandy spit protruded out into the muddy-looking lake, the river charging away on the other side. The lake looked shallow. I slithered down on to the shingly sand and waded in. The water seemed warm and I enjoyed sloshing through it. It became no deeper and I followed this sandy spit right out into the lake. I felt elated. I was saving a diversion of many miles. I was practically across! I looked back—the others were following. I was glowing with self-satisfaction when I suddenly found the ground falling away under my feet. A leafy twig tore past, indicating current. Yet the far bank was only a matter of ten feet or so away.

"Let's swim," I said to Hugh as he came up. Like me, he could not bear to go back. But I hated the thought of getting wet. I took all my clothes off and bundled them into the tent bag, which Hugh tied on to the rope. I took the other end of the rope and launched myself in. The cold clutched me, and the current swung me round, but I swam like mad, hectically thrashing my arms and kicking my feet, and my hand touched the far bank. I hauled myself out, then pulled on the rope to retrieve my clothes. But I could not do it by myself. The boys roared with laughter at my predicament. I gave up and ran about on the tundra to dry off, but without shoes I could not move fast enough to keep warm. My feet, blistered from the worn-out mukluks, were too sore on the prickly tussocks of willow and birch. My teeth chattered and I felt like Eve without her ivy.

Hugh put extra clothes on and swam slowly, having a theory that the water was warmer if you did. At last I got my clothes and the tent bag was pulled to and fro, ferrying the rest of the gear.

A belt of rocks now cut across our line, and we started to scramble up. Then we stopped, speechless. Below us was a road.

We clambered down to it, and walked up and down, feeling

the level ground beneath our feet. "Car tracks," proclaimed Roger. "Recent too." "Let's wait for a bus," I suggested, sitting down on my load. "Don't be daft," said Hugh, but he was worried. For his experiment he wanted us to "arrive" and then relax, so as to get a contrast for his hormone levels under physical stress. Ideally, the thing would be to leave our loads here, walk in to the base which must be nearby, and get a jeep to pick up the gear. "They're bound to have dozens of jeeps," said Roger. "And helicopters," added Bill hopefully.

A little black Arctic fox looked at us curiously, plucked up courage and approached boldly. Hugh broke off a precious piece of meat-bar and held it out. It ran up, as quick as lightning, but dived at the hand behind his back, and gobbled up the main block. Hugh's puzzled face contrasted with the crafty grin of the fox as it scampered off, licking its lips.

After much conversation, we decided to rely on a jeep, and walk in with as little as possible. We separated our sleeping-bags and a little food from the main pile of gear. "Won't need much," said Hugh confidently, "the boat will have been in bringing the canoes, etc., that we shipped off from Leith. I sent a spare shirt and trousers and boots." So had we all. I had sent a new toothbrush and soap, books and a hairbrush. "Hooray!" I said, leaping to my feet. "Come on. We are bound to get hospitality, so we don't need any food."

With a light load, the walk was delightful. We followed the sandy track up and down and round the undulating ground. The view behind was to the fantastically jumbled ice of the glacier. "No route across that," I thought, then remembered that we had just made one.

"Look," I said, "chewing-gum papers." Suddenly I felt reluctant to arrive, to have to meet people and talk, particularly to women. There was still no sign of life ahead, but a cone of a hill blocked our view.

"That's the Sugar Loaf," said Hugh, consulting the map. "The air strip must be just round the other side." By now it was eight in the evening. "Too late to arrive," I said adamantly. "Let's camp and get there in the morning."

"Camp?" said Bill. He was all for pushing on, but the others felt like me and longed for another night to brace us up before encountering civilisation.

A little thicket of low willow scrub bordered a tiny lake on our right. The sun was lowering behind a shoulder of hill, throwing a golden light on the water. This turned to navy blue while we chose a spot to spread our sleeping-bags, and took on a texture as the moon crept up and substituted its yellow light. Hugh and I had a little spot to ourselves, screened from the others by a higher bush. I suddenly remembered that we would be parting soon, and so our nearness seemed more precious.

Where else could one sleep out and be warm and dry? In Scotland a night without a tent always ends in disaster, the rain starting in those awful hours before the dawn. Two little birds, a cross between a gull and a miniature duck, bobbed about in the little lochan nearby when we stirred at 6 a.m. My favourite of all appeared, three red-necked phalaropes. They nod their heads like busy little women meeting in the village, and float high in the water, buoyantly like corks. They are back-to-front to other birds, the female enticing the male, who in turn hatches the eggs and tends the young. They are very tame and appeared unmoved when I walked to the water's edge. I had a marvellous feeling of freshness as I dipped my face in the silvery water and dried it on a handful of moss. Wraiths of mist hung over the lochan, giving a magical air to our delightful spot. We had our meagre breakfast round an open fire, bringing back memories of Australian days when I had wandered in the Outback, now very far away. Then it was always thick steaks we cooked—here it was a second-hand bag of tea.

"Come on," urged Bill, already on the road. His impatience to be off irritated our more reluctant spirits. The fact was, we didn't want to arrive.

The road was improving all the time. Round a corner—and

we were there! A lorry was just pulling away. Bill charged it, and it stopped. The driver spoke no English, but indicated that we could "hop on".

Two miles down the road and we juddered to a halt beside an ultra-smart wood-and-glass building. "Now what do we do?" asked Bill, as we stood around, peering through the windows. It was the airport lounge, very snazzy and smart, with civilised tourists sitting about on Danish teak chairs. I eyed the boys. We looked ghastly!

"Go and ask for the manager," I said to Hugh, putting off the moment when I had to do anything useful. Reluctantly he pushed open the door and went in. Back he came with a smooth, elegantly suited Danish gentleman, whose English was impeccable. "Good afternoon," he said, putting out his hand. I put my filthy rough one in his and he shrank visibly and didn't offer his to the boys. "Perhaps a bath?" he asked. "We can give you a room at the hotel." We exchanged glances. Not what we expected at all! To pay for hotel rooms in the depths of Greenland and something we hadn't thought of.

Hugh explained about our luggage that should have arrived by boat. The manager blanched slightly and shook his head. "The boat is lying off the harbour and has been for one week costing us Danes good money, but she cannot unload as an American boat is in. My hands are tied. I can do nothing." "Well," I suggested, "let's have the bath while Hugh tries his luck with the Americans."

*　　　*　　　*

"Hi!" said the first official American Hugh had met. "Sorry I can't offer you a beer. We are out of it—ours froze, so the M.O. condemned it. We threw it into the sea, but it was washed up and the Eskimoes got hold of it. The Danes were furious and made us gather it all up. We loaded up a helicopter and turfed it out over the ice." "I know," said Hugh. "We found it." As well as having no beer, the American had no "available" jeeps either. "Surely," Hugh stressed, looking at the fleet of U.S. vehicles plying up and down to the harbour to unload their boat, "you could lend us one. The road is good and it'll only take a few hours." "No," said the American. "I can't help either," said the manager of the hotel. "There is a shop, though, at the U.S. base where you could buy a change of clothes." Roger and I walked across the tarmac to the huddle of U.S. huts. We found the shop. My eyes widened. It had everything in it. Food-mixers, records, bras and even scent! A big, burly Yank barred our way. "Who are you? Got any dollars? We sell only to people carrying a pass." We tried to explain, to ask how to get the pass. "Oh, come on," I tugged at Roger's sleeve. "I can't bear it. Let's go back for that gear now and sleep in the tundra away from all these bloody people." And so we did.

*　　　　*　　　　*

We established our camp below the kerfuffle of the base and hotel, beside the little harbour at the head of the fjord. I knocked at the door of a hut to explain who we were while the boys pitched the tent. "Sealift for Security" was on the door. No answer. I opened it. A man sat at a desk. "Navy-Military, American-Danish liaison" was written on the wall. He had a friendly face that nearly burst with astonishment when he looked up and saw me at his door. "What can I do for you?" he asked. If only we had met him a few days before. When he heard that there were three others of me outside, he leapt to his feet to call them in.

He made us coffee and plied us with coke and butter, milk and showers. "If you need a jeep at all," he said, "I've got three."

Our priorities had changed now, the children's plane was due in a few hours. Bill stamped moodily about. I knew that he felt upset that Maureen was not to be with them on the plane. I felt guilty at my excitement. I had Hugh and the children; he had no one and another six weeks or so before he reached home. "You could leave us now, you know," said Hugh, understanding his longing to be reunited with his family. But Bill would not consider this. He felt he would be letting us down if he went home before the end of the expedition. Once his mind is made up, Bill cannot be swayed.

I kept looking at my watch and at last even Hugh agreed that it was time to go. We juddered back up the road in one of three jeeps while I kept telling myself that the children might not be there. The arrangements for their departure were so complicated that something could so easily have gone wrong between Loch Awe and Søndre Strøm.

I clutched Hugh's arm as we stood poised on the tarmac, waiting for the great jet to swoop down. "Here it comes!" I cried, choking back tears of excitement. It taxied up and came to a stop. Rows of faces at the windows. I scanned them all. No sign. Slowly and inefficiently a Greenlander in jeans pushed out the steps. I rushed to help, to hurry him up.

The usual international mob of passengers started to flow out. En route for Los Angeles, they all had to disembark for refuelling. Blank stares met my enthusiasm. Tall sophisticated Scandinavian women in leather coats. Fat men carrying buckled brief-cases. "There's my Mum!" shrieked a shrill little voice from behind me. Three figures had just exploded out of the 1st Class exit. "Why's Dad got fur on his face?" Rona's relentless little voice. I pushed aside the indignant flock of well-heeled passengers and then had to wait while the queue walked demurely down the steps, jostled from behind by the children. At last . . . I clutched them to me, burying my face in their warm, firm bodies. Bruce and I cried. He clung to my neck without a word. I could feel a mutual bond flowing between us, deeper than speech. Robin was taking everything in his stride, and Rona already had the attention of the only two men in uniform. Behind them came Heather, clutching bags, boxes, paper windmills, comics, jerseys and fishing-rods. Her huge smile and enthusiasm were a tonic, and soon we had extracted everyone and all her fourteen pieces of luggage and loaded them on to the jeep that we had borrowed from our harbour friend. I had had enough of this patch of artificial civilisation and was longing to get back to the uncluttered tundra, where the things that mattered were more fundamental.

We bumped back down the road to where we had pitched the tent above the harbour. What excitement! Letters, presents, news from home. Heather lifted the lid of a wooden crate. Peaches! "I bought them in Covent Garden this morning," she said. "I think they'll be all right." So did we! Marvellous! The downy, baby skin was heaven against my cracked lips. The juice seeped out of the firm flesh as my teeth carved their way through. "Oh delicious," I said in ecstasy, reaching for another from its nest of green shredded straw.

The children were exhausted. They had left Loch Lomond-side that very morning at 6 a.m., driven to Glasgow, flown to London alone, met Heather, then flown over to Copenhagen. "Didn't you sleep in Copenhagen Airport?" I asked. "Sleep!" exclaimed Heather. "We went to the fun fair in the Tivoli Gardens. It was good fun till I realised I was clasping the neck of a wooden horse, birling round a roundabout, and they were on quite another, sitting in an airship and going in a different direction. By the time I got off mine, theirs was whirling round again. I took a flying leap into a rocket, then found it was still the wrong one. I didn't dare get off and could see them wandering through the crowd, looking for the original wooden horse. I had just reached them when a kindly Dane lifted them on again and paid their fare. We only just made the plane!"

Heather had never before had the charge of three healthy children of two, four and five, and had learnt the hard way about the attraction of aeroplane lavatories, the irresistible urge to fiddle with the bell and ventilation buttons, and the awful remarks in a loud voice about the woman in the seat in front. Three children make a gang but Heather had obviously already become a member of it, rather than declaring war.

Our neighbour, the American in charge of the comings and

goings of the U.S. supply ships, wandered up to the tent. "A friend of mine's just flown in with some steak—we're having a barbecue here. Coming?"

Beer, four-inch-thick steaks, and newly baked bread, eaten over a smoky charcoal fire, made up for any lack of enthusiasm at the main base. "Heather is just more of an attraction than you," explained Hugh in a husbandly way. Perhaps he was right! The party moved into the hut. I sat on the American's desk and idly toyed with his various rubber stamps. "SORRY ABOUT THAT" said one in capital letters. What a treasure for a man dealing with liaison between two nations. The Americans were diplomats after all!

*   *   *

At six o'clock the following morning, we had to go. I cursed last night's party as I tried to open my eyes and think. Hugh, Bill and Roger took down the tent and carted our luggage down to the water's edge. I tried to segregate what we needed, and what was to go with the boys. Had they got all the salt and we all the pepper? Did they want the frying-pan or could we have it and the billy-can too?

"Hurry up," said Hugh, worn down with a few days' contact within range of radio and mail. He was coming with us to establish our camp, and at last we were all aboard the little boat that we had hired for the day.

"Where's all the food?" said Heather, eyeing the small pile of six weeks' luggage, for her and me and the children. "We're going to live off the land," I said brightly. "That's why you brought out the fishing-rods. Remember?" "Yes," said Heather bleakly, "but didn't you say you'd never fished?" She was quite right, I had always looked upon it as a lazy, useless sort of sport at home, and when we had been in a situation relying on fish for food, I had always left it to Hugh. "You said you were going to learn," I reminded her accusingly, "but it's easy, anyhow. Anyone can catch fish."

Twenty miles down the fjord a river had carved out a little bay, sheltered from the main fjord, with a sandy beach and grassy slopes. What more could we want for our camping holiday? As our little outboard chugged towards the shore we could see the mast of a boat, aground on the far side of the river. Behind it was an encampment. "Tinkers," said the children, thinking of Loch Lomondside. "No, its Greenlanders," I explained. "They come up here from the coast every summer to shoot reindeer. They need the meat for the winter. They dry it in strips, like the South African biltong, and then it lasts them all through the dark months when they can't get at the seal. Each family has an area that it has traditionally hunted for generations. These people we are going to meet will have come from the mouth of the fjord, a hundred miles or so away."

Should we camp with the Greenlanders? I decided not. We had our collection of plants to make, mine for the Edinburgh Herbarium and Heather's grasses for the British Museum. I knew from experience that if one has work to do, it is better to camp alone.

Behind the sandbank was a grassy ledge nestling at the foot of higher sandy dunes. Here was a delightful site for the tent. Hugh helped us lay out our gear. "Got everything?" he asked helpfully. "Heaven knows," I answered. We had spent so much time organising the equipment for the ice-cap crossing that this latter stage in the expedition had been rather left to chance.

Hugh had to go. I felt only momentarily sorry. The children meant so much more to me at the time, now that I had them again. We stood on the sandbank and the boat chugged away. "Had we forgotten anything vital?" I thought. Supposing someone got appendicitis? Perhaps there weren't any fish. Such thoughts slipped through my mind, till it was out of sight. "Hell!" I exclaimed, suddenly remembering something, "I never read the letters." Hugh had still got the lot in his rucksack. What with last night's party and the early start I had forgotten about them.

"Forgot!" said Heather indignantly. "People kept sending them, marked 'urgent' and 'reply immediately'. Did you see the envelope of telegrams?" I shook my head. I felt rather pleasantly guilty. Hugh would have to answer the lot. "I expect he thinks you've got them. I bet he doesn't look at them either," said Heather, who proved to be only too right.

Robin had already discovered the possibilities of the sand-bank and was launching himself off at the top for a grand slither to the bottom. I kept picking up Rona, kissing her fat cheeks, and hugging her to me. How could I have left them for so long?

Our first job was to catch our lunch. "Salmon-trout from the river, or cod from the fjord?" I decided on the latter, remembering Roger's remarks that "the fjords were stiff with them". I fitted together our collapsible canoe. It was broader and fatter and cheaper than the ones I had used before. They had been built on more kayak lines, like the ones that the boys had taken on their trip. I launched it, popped Bruce in the front, and lowered myself in over the canvas sides, carefully placing my bare feet on the wooden struts making the floor. I pushed off. The current picked us up. We shot out of the mouth of the river, into the quietness of the bay. It was flat calm, mirroring the rising hills. A grey old man's head bobbed up and eyed us curiously. A seal, with long whiskers and a very comic face. We drifted farther out. An agitated northern diver swept her family out of our wake, giving me an aristocratic stare.

"I've got a fish," said Bruce, but I didn't take much notice. I was absorbed in the tranquil scene. Suddenly the fragile kayak juddered and swayed. We were going backwards—out into the open fjord. Bruce clung on to his brand new rod with a desperate face. I clung on to the sides of the kayak, equally desperate. A cod had caught us. Who would win? I inched forward and grabbed the end of Bruce's rod, and between us we wound it in. We got that fish, but only just before it got us. With bleeding fingers and somewhat battered craft we returned triumphant. Heather produced from below the remaining peaches, a cucumber and a lemon. One-upmanship had reached a new score.

Our next meal ensured, we crossed the river to make friends with the Greenlanders. Soon Rona and a little boy the same size were playing "dollies" with a piece of wood, and Heather was crouching beside a weather-worn woman, beating the blue-bottles off a newly flayed reindeer skin, as she stretched it out to dry on the ground. Thin strips of meat were drying in the sun—a black crust forming on the outside, red and raw in the middle. An older woman was coiling up strips of sinew and placing them in a dried stomach—her sewing-bag. A baby peeped out over her shoulder, safe and warm in her *amout* or anorak hood. I knew just how much babies like to be carried about like this. My children had never cried when they were slung on my back in the Lapland *komse*. They loved the security of its confined space that hugged them tight, and they liked to be close to me. The *komse* swayed as I moved about, and they slept more peacefully than they ever did in a cot. I feel sorry for babies when I see them lying abandoned in their prams. How much they would prefer their parents to be un-civilised and carry them about on their backs!

Bruce was overflowing with excitement about his fish and I realised that I would just have to go back over the river and cook it before he burst. I lowered myself into the canoe, and pushed it out into deeper water while Heather rounded up the children. Rona set in the extreme front, curled up to avoid me bashing her head with the paddle. Bruce sat between Heather's feet at the back and Robin in the middle. If we overturned, the plan was for me to rescue Rona, Heather to clutch Bruce, and poor five-year-old Robin was told to "cling to the boat, or else". The Greenlanders crowded on the bank to see us off, laughing and pointing at the laden canoe. "*Umiat*," they said again and again, choking with laughter on the word. I remem-bered that this was Eskimo for the large open women's boat, as opposed to the men's stream-lined kayak. "*Umiat*," we echoed, nodding our heads, and joined in the laughter. Heather was not so sure of the joke. She thought she had bought herself a rather special canoe and there was something derogatory about an *umiat*. It implied an "old tub".

We collected flat stones to build our fireplace and discovered that the low willow scrub surrounding our camp burnt like tinder. The children gathered twigs with enthusiasm and soon we had a substantial pile. The frying-pan hissed as Heather dropped in the wedges of white, flaky fish. The smell was exquisite and I could hardly wait while Heather cut the cucumber into polite sections and squeezed the lemon on top.

Delicious. "More," said Rona, her fat cheeks bulging, and I remembered the trouble to get her to eat at home.

"Who is the best at catching fish?" asked Bruce repeatedly, glowing in the answer "You, without a doubt."

The sun was dropping slowly behind the hills at our backs, the yellow sand around us turning gold as it sunk into a belt of cloud. A stillness crept over our valley and enveloped us. The children crawled quietly into the tent and curled up in my sleeping-bag. Heather and I sat and sipped our tea. The fjord had lost all colour now, but taken on an extra dimension as if the water would be thick to the touch. The hills beyond were black—a solid band. Hugh, Roger and Bill would be behind them already, but I did not hanker to be with them. I was tired, worn out after the physical stress of the ice-cap journey. I wanted to sit, like this, and absorb the surroundings, to become part of the scene. Life is made up of contrasts, and only by having a contrast can we measure our enjoyments and pleasures. Heather, straight from her broker's office in the City, looked completely at home and I knew that we had chosen well when we had asked her to come. A lesser person would have held on to her sophisticated ways for security, but Heather was complete in herself.

A light wind fanned our cheeks and then it was cold. I crawled into the tent, and pushed the sleeping children till there was room for me in the big double sleeping-bag. "I'll take one in my bag," offered Heather, but I wanted them all.

I had been waiting a long time for tonight. I edged in between them and they snuggled up in their sleep automatically, like puppies. Robin's bony arms came round my neck in a vice-like grip and his knobbly, little boy's knees prodded me in the back. But I was happy as only a mother can be.

*   *   *

I had forgotten the irritation of being wakened up at 6 a.m. "Mummy, Mummy, I'm hungry," said Rona, prising open my eyes. But the sun was up already, and the view through the round tent door was of a glorious morning. The fjord was flat calm, broken only by the wake of a Greenlander's oars. The camp over the river was full of life, so I felt obliged to stir too. Suddenly my view was blocked by a round smiling face, then a cluster of little faces pushed and jostled to get a look in. "What is your name?" I asked the oldest, a beautiful, almond-faced girl of elevenish. I pointed to Rona, Robin and Bruce, enunciating their names. "Hansina," she replied, understanding at once. She wrote it in Heather's notebook, in an old-fashioned round hand. During the winter, the children must attend the Danish school in their district and learn to write Danish as well as their native tongue. Only recently has Eskimo been written down. It is a language unique in itself and it is said to take many years of living among Eskimoes to understand a running conversation among the locals, but we hoped to pick up enough in a short time to make ourselves understood. As their children chatted together, I began to despair of ever sorting out the continuous sound of ks and gs, but Heather was looking intelligent, and copying names into her book.

We knew that there were pitfalls; that, for instance, by knowing the word for "knife" and the word for "small" one cannot put them together and say "small knife". A different word is used, like our "pony" instead of "small horse". Eskimo has few adjectives, but numerous suffixes to add on to the noun. These can be attached one after another—perhaps six or eight—

resulting in a word of vast length. A suffix can completely change the meaning of the noun. For instance, *iglu* means a home, *iglupuk* a large home, *iglukuk* a ruined home, *igluhanga* the home that he built. All these suffixes are used in addition to the declension endings, like *iglumun*—to the house.

This is only the start; the verb is far more complicated. Endless suffixes can be added to modify its meaning; for instance *tikitpok*—he has arrived, but *tikiniakpalungwiakpaung*— will he probably arrive do you think? An Eskimo with a feeling for words can go on practically indefinitely.

The authority on the Eskimo language is Stefansson, who lived among them for many years in the 1900s. He mentions that, for an Englishman, it would be easier to learn Russian, Swedish, French and Greek than acquire Eskimo alone. However, Heather and I were prepared to try.

Robin handed the children at the door some "Happy Family" cards that Heather had given him to play with on the plane.

"Oh, *tupilaks*," they said, hands outstretched, then gazing at them intently. The picture of Mrs. Frog rocking a cradle with a tadpole inside, and Mrs. Squirrel complete with bonnet and apron, were enchanting them, but how could I explain? What would the missionaries on the coast say when our new friends told them that we went around with pictures of spirits to keep us safe? Robin was trying to show them how to play, talking louder and louder to make them understand. They thought that they did and started to scrape pictures of their *tupilaks* in the sand for comparison.

Hansina's calm face was transfixed into a magnificent smile as she gave up the game, took Rona by the hand and led her off down to the little stretch of beach within the river's bar. The other children scampered off to follow, Robin and Bruce in their midst. Hansina loaded them into a little rowing boat and pushed out. The tide was in, our estuary full and the river tamed. I could see Hansina leaning over the side. A tiny boy held her one oar and the boat swayed from side to side.

I remembered that I had said, "No one is to go into a boat without a life jacket," but I felt that I could not spoil the scene by shouting out and imposing my will on the group.

Hansina was emptying the fish net that her mother had stretched across the river. Big silvery bodies slithered out of her hands into the boat, the children shrieking with delight every time one plopped among their bare feet. Traditionally only the women fish and the Danes have had trouble persuading the men to work in their fish factories as they considered the job effiminate. Yet, deprived of their hunting lives by the modern advances of civilisation that cause the population to explode, they needed something to do, and so must be moved to employment by the Danes.

I was filling our bucket with water as Hansina sculled her boat across to our side, to re-set the net. Her little boat was made of driftwood, some pieces minute, and jig-sawed together. The sections were held in place by the outer skin, made of canvas and bits of pelt all sewn together to fit exactly the inner frame. There were no rowlocks and the oars, or rather oar, was a long pole slightly shaped at one end. The boat was completely watertight and I was surprised how light it was as I helped haul it up the beach. The fish at the bottom were Arctic char, a species of salmon-trout. "No, *ekaluk*," said Robin indignantly. Hansina handed him two, so I knelt down beside her to gut them on the spot. The children crowded round like sparrows. Hansina split her fish with a flick of her wrist, pulled out the innards with a lightning movement, and popped one bag of glistening roe into her mouth! She handed me the other. Memories of swallowing fishes' eyes when living with Australian aborigines flashed in front of me and I passed on my present to Rona, praying that she would maintain the family's obligations of social success. Smiling at Hansina, she crammed the oozy beads into her rosebud mouth and chewed happily, little round balls escaping at the corners and dribbling down to her pointed chin. All the children were now clamouring for roe and Hansina opened up the rest of her fish, throwing them the delicacy, which they shared among them, Robin and Bruce well to the fore.

These Arctic char would have moved out of our river in May to forage in the sea. But in August the fish seem to have an irresistible urge to return to the fresh-water lakes. They wait about in the bays at the river mouths, getting fat and strong and so able to cope with the strenuous migration up the water-falls and rapids between the fjord and the haven of the inland lakes. The males are beautiful, with dark heads, orange spots on their sides and bright pink underneath. When caught in the river, their stomachs were always empty as they do not eat when they migrate. The females are more silver on top and redder beneath, with the eggs ripe and ready to burst.

"Breakfast!" shouted Heather and I looked up to see blue smoke coiling up from our fire and her cheerful face framed in an untidy mop of black hair. I was suddenly struck with her similarity to our new friends. Already she looked like an Eskimo and I was beginning to feel like one too.

I felt a lightness of heart and freedom from care that was exalting as I walked back to our camp, the newly caught char in my hand. The next few meals were accounted for. What more was there to worry about?

Our collection of flowers was to be comprehensive. "I would rather have everything growing in a limited area, than a few varieties covering many miles," had said the voice of the Edinburgh Herbarium. "Where shall we start?" I asked Heather for advice as I armed myself with a long knife and a plastic bag and looked around hopefully for a colourful bloom. I descended on a little daisy-like erigeron growing in the sand. My knife bit into the ground, then came to an abrupt halt. In spite of the intense summer heat, the ground was frozen solid a few inches below.

When I lifted out the root of my plant, the layer of sand attached below it felt icy cold. I shivered, not at the cold in my hand, but at the mysterious petrified deadness just a finger's depth away. This lovely land surrounding us was so shallow.

Its light grip on the icy world frightened me. I was not big enough in myself to live in such insecure surroundings. My civilisation had taken away from me the inherent belief in self-reliance so evident in the women across the way.

The more I looked on the ground, the more growing plants I found. If I retraced my steps I always saw something that I had missed before. I had to overcome the blindness of not look-ing. A new dimension was opening at my feet, like the first time one gazes at the sea floor with a snorkel on one's face. I had always noticed flowers, but in a casual sort of way. Now I had really to concentrate, to be able to write down the differ-ence between this little white flower and that. This one always grew in the sand at sea-level, but on scree if we found it higher up, while that one grew only in sand at all altitudes. I became so interested that I was cross when Rona interrupted me, sitting on the plant I was about to dig up. "I'm hungry—what about our tea." I looked at my watch. Hours had passed by. Where were the boys? And Heather?

"Over there," said Rona, pointing down to the river's edge. I hoisted Rona on to my shoulders and galloped down the sandbank. I could hear shrieks of delight. Heather and the boys were bathing. In behind the river's bar was a steep sand dune nearly covered at high tide, but now the receding tide had left a sheltered bay. The two little boys were pushing each other down the steep bank into the water, sand and mud plastering their pink bodies, in their hair and over their faces. They were vying to see who could make the loudest splash, who would go the deepest, who could brave the cold enough to actually lie down. Heather was prancing in and out too.

"Why don't you swim out into the deep water?" I asked, throwing off my clothes. I put in one leg. The water was warm! I launched out and realised why Heather had gone no deeper. The cold gripped me in a vice. I couldn't breathe. Hastily I turned round and joined the other in the shallows. Here it was glorious. The sun reflected off the sand, and the warmth seemed to soak into my tired bones.

"What a place," murmured Heather, lying flat out in the sand. "I'm unwinding already and I left the office only twenty-four hours ago." "Heather, Heather!" shouted Robin, "come and race me down the bank." She stirred at once and joined in the splashes and shrieks. Like an old grandmother I sat in the sun and looked on, too tired to move. Had the ice-cap drained my energy for ever, or could I replenish it, like a camel, in the peace of our pastoral life here?

Rona chivvied us back to the tent for food. Fried, till the skin was crisp and golden, the Arctic char was delicious. There was plenty of juicy flesh, and the bones were easy to remove. A squeeze of Heather's lemon, a pinch of salt and pepper, and they tasted better than anything you could buy at home.

A cluster of children joined us again and Heather handed out paper and pencils for drawing. The fair- and black-haired heads intermingled closely as they bent over, intent. Hansina drew a lonely and remote house, lurking at the foot of enormous mountains that filled most of the page, dark and forbidding. She blackened them in. She gazed at her drawing for some time, then carefully added one solitary figure, poised and alone. Two of the boys drew fishing-boats, nets bulging with the catch, and one boy pin men figures running after an animal, full of the excitement of the chase. "*Tugtoo, tugtoo*," said Bruce, and the children laughed, then rolled him on the ground, tumbling on top, playing like puppies and little boys the world over, sparring for a playful fight.

A *tugtoo* was a reindeer, now the Greenlanders' staff of life. In the old days, seal, walrus and bear were frequent enough to provide protein for the population of Greenlanders that were then alive. The men hunted with spears and harpoons and so the animals stood a fair chance of not being killed, of living to provide a meal in a year or two hence, after having a few babies to maintain the species in between. But the white man came and brought his gun and the mass slaughter began. European man seems incapable of learning from experience and the tragedies are re-enacted the world over where he imposes his way of life on the perfectly happy and stable primitive societies that existed long before his ancestors were born.

There is no game now for the people of south and central Greenland, except the reindeer, and these have been recently reintroduced. There are a few musk-ox, but a heavy penalty awaits the man who shoots one. The modern Greenlander, of course, does not have to hunt. He could live off the local Danish Trading Company store, which has tins of corned beef and Danish garden peas. But he would then have to own money in order to buy. To do this, he would have to take a job in the Danish fish factory and many of the Greenlanders do. But, as we now knew, some preferred the old life. The best of the Greenlanders are not to be found in the settlements or the coast, living in the Government houses, but in places like this, where they still live as their forefathers did and so have maintained not only the ways of the hunt, but such things as showing honesty, hospitality and friendship, that are far older in the world of the Eskimo than Christianity.

I suddenly realised the pressures on a hunter's life when the children remembered that they were hungry again and we now had no fish left. It is only when hunting for the pot that one appreciates how much food people eat.

"I want to try and catch an *ekaluk* in the river," said Heather, picking up her nice new, but borrowed rod. "Where is the tin of worms that the children were to dig up in Loch Awe?" I asked. "We didn't dig them," said Robin, "there weren't any at Loch Awe, so Cis and Alex had to get up early to dig them up before they put us on the plane in Glasgow." "Heavens!" I thought, visualising the scene and imagining the remarks of the friends who had the job of collecting the children from Argyll and sending them off to Heather, four hundred and fifty miles away in London. Robin dug in his bag and produced a little tin. There was a scuffling noise from inside. "You open it," said Heather generously. "No, you," I insisted, drawing back. Robin prised off the lid, and held it under my nose. The writhing wriggling mess made me turn away with horror.

"Look, Mum," said Robin enthusiastically, "here is a nice one." "Give it to Heather," I said, "I'm prepared to live off cod. You don't need any bait for them." "We musn't be silly," said Heather in the voice of a suffragette, and marched off towards the river, clutching her rod and the tin. But she launched our *umiat* and set off into the fjord after the cod.

Unfortunately, having tasted Arctic char, the cod was a poor substitute. Heather dug in the bottom of the borrowed fishing-bag and emptied out reels and exotically coloured flies. "Sweeties," said Rona, her eagle eyes falling on a little packet. "Sickorus," she said, as she opened it up and took a bite. Suddenly I noticed the label and grabbed it back. "Pickled bait. Best salted worms, guarantee a catch." I wondered what the makers would say if we sent a picture of Rona, chewing happily on what she thought was liquorice.

I walked up the river to where it turned a corner, leaving a deep dark pool. I attached a piece of pickled worm, swung my arm, and the spinning reel allowed it to plop gently into the mysterious depths. Immediately I saw a shape. The rippling silver of an Arctic char! It couldn't resist my fortified worm, and bit heavily on to the hook. I had never wound in a fish in a river before and I was surprised at the strain on my arm as it swung to and fro, determined to get free. All my kindly instincts vanished in a second, and I was determined to get that fish. To catch it and kill it and eat it. The bank was steep so I had to take it up-stream to a little bay where at last I could lift it ashore. It lay heaving at my feet. I extracted my hook and stood up to admire the fish. One flick of its tail and it was back in the water, one wriggle of its and body and away it went. I was astonished. Robin interrupted me, shouting. "He's drowning," I thought, throwing down my rod and running back down the bank. He was jumping about at the river's edge screaming for me, his rod bent to a ghastly angle, and a big silver body on a tight line hurling itself to and fro. I knelt down, put my hands underneath and scooped it out, throwing it several yards up the bank.

Robin was ecstatic. Little boys just love to be important, to help maintain the family, and what could be better than this? He, of course, had not used any bait, just spun out his reel and cast his line with its silvery spinner attached. How could I break it to Alec and Cis that we didn't need their worms? Or Heather's stockbroker friend and his pickled ones?

"Look," said Heather, coming up. A boat was coming over to our side, with a gang of youths aboard. Five big boys of about seventeen got out, laughing and joking, then came towards us in a silent, sinister group. I drew nearer to Heather, and looked about for Rona and Bruce. One is so instilled with reports of teenage violence and gangs in Glasgow that I was frightened as they advanced. One was carrying something behind his back. Was it a knife? They stopped a little short of us and stood looking ominous. Now what?

"Ignore them," I thought, and cleaned my fish. One came up, grabbed it, then ran off, towards our tent. The rest moved too and hoisted the children on to their shoulders, and gambolled off into the scrub, Bruce and Robin yelling with delight. Suddenly I felt ashamed. "They had come to bring us a present," said Heather, as we reached our camp and the big one handed me a haunch of meat.

Quickly we made tea and handed it round and I tried to make up for my evil thoughts. The big boy was now lying with Rona bouncing on his stomach and Robin covering his head with sand.

One was looking at the flowers waiting to be pressed, and joined Heather as she laid them carefully out on the blotting paper. He picked up her pencil and wrote out the names.

Heather was overjoyed. The boys were thrilled that we were interested in their language, and knew all the names. Unlike me, Heather has a brilliant brain, and can retain information like this, remembering the Eskimo words. The boys told her the words she wanted to know and quickly understood why she insisted on spelling them as pronounced. They thought this funny and the noise of their laughter echoed in our bay.

Angujartorfik it was called, and the boys were pleased with Heather's pronunciation. Mine, they said, was bad, and they all laughed again.

Eskimoes are a happy, optimistic race. There is no room for a pessimist in the Arctic. A fatalistic worrying outlook has been the cause of death of many an explorer. Greely's men never expected to live through another winter, and they did not, dying one by one, while Greely himself lived to tell the tale, as he always said he would. Scott did not expect to win through, the last entries in his diary being full of impending death. Courtauld, on the other hand, "knew" that all would be well, and Mylius Eriksen's optimism got them through incredible situations of starvation and cold. The Eskimo copes with today's dangers and difficulties, doing the best that he can, and gives no thought to tomorrow except that it will take care of itself, like yesterday did. They enjoy life and are happy, and when anything goes wrong laugh at the joke that circumstances has played on them.

I asked the boys about the birds, showing them pictures and illustrations from my book that Heather had brought out. They knew them all. "Snowy owl?" I asked, longing to see one. '*Ugpik*" they said, but shook their heads; not here. Plenty, where their homes were at Kangamiut on the coast and farther north. I asked them about the little auk, which was nearly killed off because the Eskimoes used them to make their winter shirts. They used to be captured in nets, one hundred and fifty needed for one shirt. The skins were first dried, then chewed by the women, until all the oil was extracted and the skin was soft and pliable and ready to sew. The boys knew all about this, but were quite adamant that no one in their district did this now, except for the Americans.

"Americans?" said Heather and I, incredulous. "Yes," we interpreted the answer, the Americans at the Søndre Strøm base would pay £10 for a shirt of little auk skins, but few people bothered to go to the trouble. Money seemed to be of little importance to the Greenlanders whom we met. If they wanted a new gun they could work easily at the fish factory until they earned enough. Long live the fish factories, I thought, as I looked at the picture of the dear little auk. How the wheel has turned. Eskimoes in horrid blue jeans and Americans in feathered shirts!

The sun was sinking again, another day gone by. Identical to the last, yet totally different. The sun lingered just below the horizon, lighting up the sky with a mass of marvellous colouring. Oranges, russets, there were not enough words to cover the variation on red that were splashed in our sky by that evening light. The colours blended from bright red to saffron, purple and gold. The world stood still, a silence brooded over our valley, everyone holding their breath, mesmerised by the glory in the sky.

Then a dark curtain fell and shut off all warmth and light. The mournful call of a golden plover broke into the silence— so heartrending that tears came to my eyes and I hustled the children into bed. We joined them soon, and as I lay snuggled up in my sleeping-bag, gloriously comfortable on my kampa-mat, and warmed by the three little bodies at my sides, I looked out of the circular door of the tent into the face of the moon. It was near the earth, silvery, hanging in a navy-blue sky, dotted with stars of a brilliancy I had never seen before. It was magic. One star fell, then another, leaving streaks of light across the sky. Then they vanished. It was too beautiful to sleep.

Heather started to talk. She spends a great deal of time and energy working at the Conservative Central Office in London and was primed up with the latest political opinions. I am not now usually roused by politics, but sometimes I am incensed. When Scotland is spoken of as if it were a rather poor country in the north, I get furious: to many people in London, Scotland appears to be just that, its one usefulness being that there is plenty of room for a holiday if one does not like a crowded beach.

"What are the Conservatives going to do about the dying shipyards on the Clyde?" I asked Heather. "I think their policy would be that Scotland should be a lung for the over-populated south. A breathing space if you like," she answered, little realising that this would go to my head. I was so furious that I could not argue with her, but just issue a tirade against the "bloody English". Yet I know full well that most of my friends are English because the complacency of the average Scot drives me mad. I like people to have life and vitality, and an awful lot of this has been drained from Scotland by absentee landlords and London-centralised governments.

We talked the night out. Light was creeping back into the sky before I fell asleep, thinking that, envious as I am of my London friends and their sophisticated, geared-up lives, I was glad that it is Scotland that we would be returning to.

Early next morning our peace was shattered by the roar of an engine. "A plane, a plane," shrieked Robin and Bruce. The great black body came roaring down the valley, then with a fantastic swoosh landed in the bay. It was a seaplane. A boat was lowered from its innards and chugged its way across and beached itself on our shore. Out clambered eight men, expensively dressed "sportsmen" in waterproof trousers and tweed hats, clutching fishing-rods and canvas bags. There was no doubt as to their nationality. American voices cut the clear air.

They clambered up the bank and came towards our tent. Without saying a word to us, they clustered round, chatting together. Heather and I happened to be scraping blue-bottle eggs off our haunch of reindeer meat, as we had seen the women over the river. "Gee, here's a cute one," said a Yank, clicking his camera in Heather's face.

Blind fury rose in my throat, then sank as I saw the joke. We stifled our giggles and sat solemnly while the Americans photographed us from all angles. Heather then turned to me and spoke a sentence or two in French. One sportsman dug in his pocket and handed her a cigarette. "Look at these fair-haired children," said one. "I hope it was a Danish sailor and not a G.I. We had better check up on security." "Poor little kids," another said and handed out fistfuls of chewing-gum and candy.

Apparently they were all generals or V.I.P.s and this was an afternoon's break in a world tour of U.S. bases overseas. They spent twenty minutes at the river's edge, then hurried back to their boat, firmly convinced that they had seen something of a genuine "Eskimo" way of life. They triumphantly held the fish that they had lifted "sportingly" out of the river.

"Look!" shouted Heather, doubling up with laughter, "their boat has broken down." Sure enough it was drifting back towards our shore, while a soldier standing at the back hauled away at the string attached to the outboard motor. With mischief in her eye, Heather pushed off our canoe and quickly paddled out to them, now stuck in the sandbanks in our bay. The Greenlanders were also out for some sport and our boy friends shot out of the mouth of the river too, crowded into Hansina's little boat. I had seen these boys handling boats in expert fashion, but now I watched a hilarious scene while they played the fool. They pretended to take the U.S. boat in tow, then the boy holding the rope fell overboard, with shrieks of delight. Heather joined in, and the poor Americans sat frostily, separated from their big, powerful plane by two hundred yards of icy water, and no oars aboard to row.

Heather, straight from her office in the City, laughed the most. She had behind her two university degrees and a life of sophistication, but because of her able, broad mind, she could turn it to living successfully with our primitive new Eskimo friends. They knew that she was genuinely interested in their way of life, wanting to learn from them, not to preach. Already she had a notebook full of Eskimo words and had mastered enough to carry on a basic sort of conversation. I could never have found a better person as a companion for this stay in the tundra of the west coast or one who could have warmed the hearts of our Eskimo friends more.

As the glorious clear, calm, sunny days of August slipped past we collected the varieties of alpine plants growing in our valley, and pressed them carefully between blotting paper. The Arctic summer is desperately short and already autumn was creeping in. Most of the blooms were over, making it more exciting when we found a delicate plant still in flower, perhaps lurking under a moraine boulder, or in a crack at the back of a grassy ledge. Shoots and buds for next year were now ready, as the plant would lie dormant under the winter's snow waiting to burst into life in the following spring.

I enjoyed the excuse to wander slowly along the river bank and then sit down on a tuft of sea pinks to get a closer look at some moss. I have never been satisfied to be so lazy in my life, reaction I supposed from the physical stress of the previous months. I was glad to have the excuse of the flowers.

"Have we got this?" Heather would ask, handing me a stalk of grass. It looked the same as the other twenty we had just laid out in the sun, but we put it in as well. "Just in case." The Greenland children were more helpful than ours at turning the blotting paper over to dry. Robin preferred to fish. He would stand just in from the river's mouth, casting his line, returning inevitably with a big fat fish.

"*Ekaluk* again," he would say, trying to sound casual and adult instead of a little boy thrilled to the core. A smile would escape, and he would throw himself at Heather or me for a hug and a wet kiss. "Read us a story," Bruce would beg and Heather would reach for *Paddington Bear*. He might have come from Darkest Peru but I'm sure the author never knew that he would get to such depths in Greenland. Heather and I enjoyed the story as much as the boys. Rona was a bit frightened at the thought of a bear in the home and sucked her blankin for comfort.

Sadly we realised that Heather's time was nearly up. We had arranged that the boat would come for her on September 5th. We all piled into the *umiat* to go over to say goodbye to Hansina and her family on the far side. They were packing up too. The old Grandfather showed us the meat stacked up in the boats, enough to last them till the sun returned next spring. The younger hunters were down from the hill, and busy now rolling up the skins and stacking the dried fish at the water's edge, ready to ferry out to the bigger boat now lifted by the tide and waiting, ready to go. The women had bundles of stonecrop, a little plant with thick leaves that grew up our glen. They would pickle it in seal oil, explained one of our boy friends, and eat it during the "long night".

The old Grandfather was cleaning his gun, getting it ready to pack away. With pride he showed us the inscription on the barrel: "1917—Lee Enfield". The butt was carefully carved to fit his shoulder and cheek but we could not understand in what campaign he had won it. He was always interested by Heather's notebook of vocabulary and now took it from her hand. He shook his head over her words, saying to the boys that the spelling was wrong. Of course, it was carefully written out for pronunciation, but there was no getting round the old man. He ticked off the boys for not putting Heather right, then swept Heather's rubber across the page. He sat down and laboriously re-wrote the words in impeccable but impossible Eskimo.

The Greenlanders' boats were low in the water when they set off on the ebbing tide. They were weighed down with the winter's meat and enough fish too. As the boats passed the bar at the edge of our bay, the boys stood in the prow and shot their guns into the air—a token of farewell.

Heather left the next day. I was alone with my children.

It was a cold bleak evening and for the first time, rain was in the air. I lit the primus in the tent and we huddled inside. A few hours later, Robin looked out. "There's a shaggy animal with a cross face," he said. I glanced up. Heavens—a musk-ox. It stood a few yeards away, immobile, but fixing me with a small beady eye. It looked so prehistoric that I expected a caveman to come past, dragging his wife by the hair.

A lone bull is a dangerous thing—in any animal, including man! This one looked friendly enough but also curious. He stepped with his large feet over the guy ropes of the tent, then stood astride our fireplace, nosing my precious boxes of flowers. I was frightened. I couldn't stay in the tent, knowing that at any moment a horn might be thrust through the thin canvas between us and him. There was only one thing to do. Move. A musk-ox belongs to the sheep family and I had read that it did not like wetting its feet. We must cross the river.

Of course, it was pouring with rain. A cold wind whipped waves over the bar into our little bay. I got out first and tried not to look over my shoulder as I picked up all three children at once and attempted to walk down to the beach. "Why are we going?" protested the children. "See that friendly furry animal. Let's give it something to eat." I tried not to break into a run. Robin slipped from under my arm. "I'm going back for my rod," he said, ambling off into the willow scrub. "Never mind, Mum," said Bruce, "I'll make a burglar face to scare it away if you don't like it." Frantic now, I threw the younger children into the kayak, grabbed Robin and hauled him back. The musk-ox was on the move! The tide was out—the *umiat* far up on the beach. With all my strength I heaved the frail little boat over the sand and pushed it out into the water. Do musk-ox swim? I didn't know. I paddled hysterically across the mouth of the river—and grounded on a sandbank. Jumping out, I sank to my knees in oozy mud. Quicksands! Terrified of upsetting the boat, I tried to haul my legs free.

It seemed hours before we reached the far side. I plonked the three children down on the sand in the rain. I had to go back for the tent and sleeping-bags. The musk-ox was now pacing the river bank. It took all my nerve to land again and fetch the tent. The pegs were well in and a row of stones had to be flung off the walls. I tugged and tugged at it till it was free, then tore back to the kayak, now awash with the incoming tide. A few seconds later and it would have been away. The children were crying, complaining, with the rain. They didn't see why I had moved us from our nice camp and I did not like to frighten them with stories of wild beasts. They seemed rather to like the look of the musk-ox—it was only I who was shaking with fear.

I pitched the tent where Hansina's had been and set the boys to remove the pile of decaying fish heads and bones.

Next day broke before we were organised and another little

boat chugged in round the corner from the fjord which it had
followed up from the coast. A round little man with an elfin
face was at the helm. "Jacob," he said as he came ashore, and
clasped my hand. His wife was larger, with a friendly smile
from the heart. Magdalena was her name. We shook hands and
kissed both cheeks. Magdalena's mother was there, called
Augustina. Their three little children rushed up to mine and
from then on we were one family. They pitched their skin and
canvas tent alongside ours. I tried to help but the complications
were beyond explanation. A big stone had to go here, a smaller
one there, and a row of tiny ones at the back. Their boy of
seven knew exactly what to do and was obviously an important
member of the family.

The tent up, Jacob immediately set off up the hill, his gun
over his shoulder. Magdalena was left to fix the fish net across
the river and carry up the skins for the sleeping shelf that she
made at the back of the tent. She raised this part by gathering
stones and building them up with sticks on top. Meanwhile,
Granny picked armfuls of willow leaves and strewed them on
the sticks before laying out the reindeer pelts, hairy side up.

She invited me into her tent and I knew that this was a
compliment, that she wanted my company. She had a broken-
down primus, and to my surprise it roared into life and soon
boiled the old tin can. Meanwhile Magdalena wrapped some
coffee beans in a piece of cloth and beat it between two stones.
She emptied the ground coffee into the can, popped a slab of
"spek" or seal fat on top, and our drink was ready. She carefully wiped a cup with the wing of a bird and filled it up with
the brew. She handed me a lump of sugar and I knew how to
hold it between my front teeth and sup my coffee through. My
new friend then handed me an egg, pale blue with darker spots.
My heart sank. Duck. It must have been laid last June! Sure
enough, I saw Magdalena's jaws working on hers and when I
broke mine into my mouth I felt the softy body of an embryo
chick. My teeth ground on the gristly beak.

Although Magdalena was big for an Eskimo, she was only

as tall as me. There was a frosty nip in the autumn air, yet she stepped off their open boat in only a thin blouse and jeans. I had on two jerseys. The Eskimoes have shorter, chunkier feet, the nose does not protrude so far from the face, the hands are thicker, their fingers shorter and therefore are built to withstand intense cold better than us Europeans, and certainly this built-in insulation seems to work.

The children now were sliding down the sandbank, much steeper on this side. With a squeal of delight, Magdalena rushed off to join in, throwing herself off at the top and slithering down at breakneck speed. Old Granny pushed past me, skimmed up the bank and joined in too, shouting like the children, who adored the adults' company. "Come on, Mum," shouted Bruce. "It's great fun." So I slithered down behind the Granny, Magdalena at my back, legs and hair flying, the crystal air sweeping past our faces, sand in our eyes, and the children having the happiest day of their life.

At last energy flagged, and I could drag the children in for bed. "Gertrude too," said Rona, holding the hand of the little round-faced child with snotty nose and black, unkempt hair. She smiled at me, so how could I refuse? Robin and Bruce and Rona snuggled into my big sleeping-bag, Gertrude, Kerstinak and the boy, Pok, slithered in as well, and they piled up, giggling and laughing and hugging each other, the best of friends.

Augustina beckoned me into their tent and I had to accept. There was no room for me here! The two women stripped completely, which was more than I intended to do, and wrapped themselves in deer skins before lying down on the shelf. They lay as close as possible to each other, and as the chill of night crept up on us I drew into the huddle too.

The Greenlanders don't sleep at night—just the odd nap. The primus is kept on all the time, and the coffee-pot permanently on the boil. Endless conversations drifted on till the sun was again high in the sky. I rolled over to catch up on some sleep when Augustina went out to empty the fish net. Magdalena got up too and when I stirred a big black pot was on a stick fire, full of boiling fish. Magdalena lifted it on to the ground and the children gathered round, picking out a fish and sucking off the flesh. Robin and Bruce were completely at home and thought this an excellent way of having a meal. Augustina picked out choice bits and popped them into the open mouths of Gertrude or Rona alternately. Suddenly there was a call from the hill.

"Ahee!" shouted Magdalena, and her call echoed and re-echoed from valley to cliff and back again. She darted into the tent to pick up a little coil of rope and ran off up the hill, Pok following close behind. Soon Jacob arrived, carrying nothing, not even his gun. He looked very tired and threw himself down beside the fire, and was snoring in an instant.

I could see Magdalena and Pok coming back slowly now and I set off to meet them. Magdalena was trotting, a neat bundle on her back with four stiff legs sticking out. A gralloched reindeer stag. Pok also had a bundle, held on his back by a piece of rope across his forehead. I beckoned to him that I would take his load. The little boy, not much bigger than Robin, slipped it off his back and ran happily after his mother. I put my arms under the load, and heaved, I could not lift it. I could not even raise it off the ground. I looked around helplessly, then had the inspiration of dividing it in two. Even so, I could hardly walk and Magdalena had run, with four or five times the load. When at last all of Jacob's kill was in the camp, our work began.

Rona and oval-eyed Gertrude spent all day digging a hole. Covered in sand they both looked grey, all racial identifications lost under the grime.

The days sped past. Meals were fish or reindeer. No knives or forks, or plates to wash up. What a convenient uncomplicated life they lived and I was adapting more and more to theirs. Magdalena and I were busy all day, dissecting the animals that Jacbo had killed. The legs we threw in the river to keep fresh, the fillet steaks we ate now, the rest of the meat we cut into strips to dry for the winter and the offal we cooked for our meals. The tongue we smoked. Every single bit of reindeer was used.

Magdalena's favourite dish was to chop up slices of liver, pop them into the revolting mess that was fermenting in the stomach, leave to simmer for an hour or two to give the digestive juices a chance, then fish them out again and eat with relish. Robin loved this too, but I didn't dare try. I now liked my coffee with a slice of fat floating on the top—it satisfied my craving for butter—and the children adored raw marrow. The berries were ripe and the char flocking into the river. What more could we want?

I walked by myself one morning along the top of the sand-bank. The children were all below on the beach, rolling and laughing in the sand. Suddenly, hundreds of geese swung into view, black in a silvery sky. They were heading up our glen, due south. A few honks, and they were off to Europe. Perhaps to feed on the stubble fields in the west coast of Scotland on their journey farther south. It was a glorious calm morning. The water had a texture. There was a misty blueness on the distant hills. Our valley was golden and red. There was a dusting of new snow on the tops, a feeling of excitement and clearness in the air. I could see Jacob now, standing up in his little boat, rowing it forward, towards his nets. Magdalena was shouting to me to come for coffee. I ran down and joined her. We lay like Romans, on reindeer skins, and drank the thick syrupy liquid through sugar lumps held in our teeth. Magdalena spoke no word of English, my Eskimo was very slight, yet the companionship that flowed between us was absolutely complete. We were drawn closely together by the shared bond of human sympathy, the love of our children and our surroundings.

That evening Bruce shouted to me that "the stars had melted in the sky". I looked out of the tent to see sheets of silvery light sweeping across the sky to the east. The Northern Lights! I led Robin and Bruce up to the top of the bank and gazed speechless at the magic in the air. The lights swept the sky, rising and falling.

The sun hung lower in the sky each day and winter was on it way. What had happened to Hugh? It was now well on into

September. One morning I was squatting on the ground with Magdalena and Jacob sucking boiled *ekaluk* off the bones. Suddenly we heard screams from the children. We leapt to our feet—a blue kayak was sailing past the sandbank sheltering our bay. Hugh! He looked like the wild man from Borneo, with a great bushy beard and a great thatch of hair.

We tore down the bank, Magdalena as thrilled as I. The children waded in and propelled the battered canvas craft to our landing place below the tents. Jacob helped him ashore, while Magdalena and I clutched each other and cried. Even in the tension of the moment, I felt the honour they were doing me in identifying their family with mine.

We threw another *ekaluk* into the pot, and more coffee on the boil. Hugh never queried the situation, and squatted on the ground beside Jacob while we handed out choice bits of the pink fleshy fish, then chose a nice fresh slab of fat to swim on the top of the coffee.

The Greenlanders are affectionate people and Magdalena sat on Jacob's knee to fondle his face, and only then could I ask Hugh about his trip.

VIII

THE CANOE JOURNEY

by Hugh Simpson

(see map facing page 97)

AFTER SEEING MYRTLE, Heather and children encamped at Angujartorfik, it was time for me to say goodbye to the family for the longest time ever. Lumps stuck in my throat as we rejoined the launch to go back to Søndre Strømfjord. We had always gone on expeditions together and shared excitements; now life seemed selfish and empty. But there was no question of them coming; it was far too dangerous and Myrtle knew this as well as I. The launch now turned the corner out of Angujartorfik into the main Søndre Strømfjord. The final break had been made and now my thoughts went entirely on the plans for our journey.

The main difficulty of the canoe journey was to come soon after the start. To carry out our plans we would have to descend a large Isortoq river—possibly the largest in Greenland—for thirty-five miles. Would the waves be too large in the rapids? What if we overturned? What if the canoes were wrecked? Since the area is uninhabited we would have to be entirely self-sufficient. After the river stretch came open exposed sea-fjords; what if there was a week of bad weather? How would the food last out? Was it worth taking a tent? It seemed rather significant that on this major journey rescue equipment such as flares would be superfluous and once upset the water would kill one off so quickly that life jackets would only be of psychological benefit. But we took them all the same.

At last all the gear was ready and we began laboriously backpacking the first load from Søndre Strømfjord wireless station off northwards into the remote tundra interior. In all there was three hundred and fifty pounds of canoes and provisions and

159

this meant relaying and so covering the ground three times. The sun shone down out of a clear blue sky. The air was quite still and a swarm of flies circled around our perspiring foreheads. Underfoot the mossy ground was dry and spongy, sapping the strength of our strides. We had hoped to pull the canoes on a trolley with bicycle wheels; in fact the contraption collapsed ignominiously after a hundred yards. It was obvious that this venture had suffered because we had concentrated on our exhaustive planning for the ice-cap trip. We did not even have a proper canoe repair outfit and had to rely on some office type sticky paper tape bought at the U.S. canteen stores the day before to patch up any holes.

But we were tremendously fit after the ice-cap and had a good rest in the air base. It didn't seem long before a mile was covered and the first lake reached. The canoes were floated and the gear stowed thankfully under bow and stern. With one thrust of the paddles the streamlined craft glided almost effortlessly through the calm, cool water, leaving the frustrated flies far behind. At once we felt alive again. The far bank was soon reached and we were ready for the first night.

There was plenty of scrub wood to make a fire and soon Bill had some trout—a gift from the air base—sizzling in the frying-pan. We had a long lingering cup of cocoa, revelling in the peace of life away from the air base. There was no need for the tent; we just rolled out our sleeping-bags on the soft carpet of moss and flowers. I lay on my back and soon felt the cosy warmth that brings early sleep. A large fat old reindeer stag came down to drink in the mirror calm lake and there was also a duck family and a small collection of phalaropes. A great northern diver called in the distance. I could not imagine a better heaven. I fell asleep.

Only a short time had passed when I was rudely awoken by a crunching noise; a cheeky Arctic fox was chewing over our old fish bones only a few inches from my head. Angry at the intrusion I slung a stick at him and he vanished into the twilight.

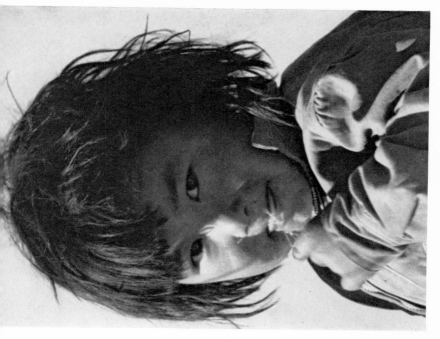

Greenlander Gertrude, Angujartorfik

Eskimo Magdalena, Angujartorfik

Greenland
child in
family tent

Gertrude and
Rona

Eskimo mother
mending one
of our Hawick
sweaters

Robin and
Magdalena

Robin welcomes Hugh back from hunting trip with Eskimoes. Hugh has reindeer carcass on his back, wrapped in its skin, and ptarmigan in his hand

Jacob: Hugh's Eskimo hunting-friend

Reindeer tongues out to dry for the winter

Counting the biscuits:
Roger on the canoe trip

Isortoq gorge: Roger battling with the current

Bill canoeing in Disko Bay

The country between Søndre Strømfjord and the Isortoq river is dotted with lakes and little hills. By detouring to use as many lakes as possible we kept the laborious portages at a minimum. The extra distance was easily covered in the canoes. Several days passed of paddling across those delightful lakes— sometimes only two stone-throws across—and short portages. The constant change of method made the ground pass quickly. Few reindeer were about but one day we saw a hare. One evening we were haunted for hours by a strange cry coming from a nearby cliff; could it be a raven or a great northern diver? Very curious I went to investigate and found a fox standing on the moraine at the foot of the crag. Every few minutes it threw back its head and let out a long eerie howl. The haunting part of the call was due to an echo off the face. It was a vixen calling for a mate and though we often heard this call in the distance, I never got used to it.

After three days, the easy canoeing came to an end. Ahead, the gentle undulating hill country was cut in two by a deep gash. We had reached the great Isortoq gorge. As we descended down a side valley we could see that the whole of the main valley was just a mass of moving opaque freezing water—the summer spate was at its height. All of us became apprehensive. Life now became a sort of automatic existence until we determined just how dangerous it was.

We floated the canoes into a quiet backwater and carefully packed everything in plastic bags; life-jackets were checked and buoyancy bags fully inflated. All of us were tense as we scanned the first rapids with binoculars. The main stream was deflected by a point of rock and for a hundred yards there was a mass of white water. The massive size of the river seemed overwhelming and I have never seen such a fast current, even in a glacier river. Would the turbulent water swamp the delicate craft? In our pockets we carried emergency dehydrated meat and matches but all of us knew an overturn would be fatal. For one thing the far shore was no haven as there was nowhere to walk to. How long could one stay alive on blueberries, I wondered? In any event this icy water would surely finish one off pretty fast. Should we turn back? If the others had suggested this I would not have said no.

Roger went off first in the single canoe and we anxiously watched his progress through the binoculars. Once out of our backwater bay his craft was gripped in the axis of the current. Any paddling he made seemed utterly feeble compared with the power of the current. He was irresistibly drawn into the worst turbulence and the tiny craft was almost lost from sight in the standing waves. We could see only his head. Soon it would be our turn. My heart thumped at the prospect.

Roger now appeared beyond the rapids and with the binos we saw his "thumbs-up" sign. As far as he was concerned the steepness of the gorge already made retreat impracticable.

Bill pushed off our double canoe. Soon the bank was going past at tremendous speed. I felt rather exhilarated. Then I saw the massive standing waves racing up to meet us. Helplessly we headed straight for the biggest ones—great walls of white-capped brown water. The water was all round us, pouring into the cockpit. But the very speed of our descent was saving us from being swamped. We were now gripped by the multiple eddies behind the point. The rudder had little effect and the craft felt hideously unstable. But we managed to slice through the great whirlpools into calm water. Roger's cheery figure appeared on the bank and soon we joined him. The first bogy was past. We had done one mile. Thirty-four still remained. Would the current ease off as we descended? Anyway it couldn't get any worse.

Now at close quarters on the bank, the rapids were very impressive. The standing waves looked a hopeless proposition because of their sheer size and shape. Often in a smooth stretch of water they would appear, rise to a crescendo, then suddenly subside. They seemed to be formed by the current gouging out a furrow of sand until the whole system became top heavy and collapsed.

Ferocious rapids came every mile or so and the most frightening of all were the ones behind precipices which we could not investigate. Then it was a question of hoping for the best since the current made it utterly impossible to paddle back upstream. After five miles of this river I felt absolutely exhausted and since there was a little flat ground at the bank I was quick to suggest an early camp. It seemed we had done little but the continuous strain had left me utterly played out. As we fell asleep there was little comfort in the fact that thirty miles of the river still remained to be done. Roger, as always, remained apparently unmoved by the river dangers and was extremely competent in his canoe. Billy had done little canoeing before and I think comforted himself that since Roger and I thought it all right we would win through. To me the margin of safety seemed to be so miserably small—travelling like an express train but with the river current, as it were, dominating the controls completely and sucking one inevitably into the worst water.

The next morning was fine and after a few minor rapids we made ten easy miles to a side channel. Even here the current was very swift, but since the river was wider and the water shallow we were able to relax. We stopped for a prolonged lunch and had a good feast of blueberries while some reindeer grazed happily close above. More side channels led us on and we soon found that the hazard was in going aground. The side channels had infinite numbers of tributaries, distributaries and in the turbid opaque water it was almost impossible to gauge the depth. When the canoe went aground it was swept quickly broadside to the current and threatened to capsize on the ridges of sand underneath. Then one of us would jump out, to be met by quicksand that gripped boots like a vice. But all these difficulties were trivial by comparison with earlier hazards, and by evening we had done a full fifteen miles.

Now that the river was easier one was able to gaze up at the great walls that lined the gorge. It was a classical glacial valley. Great successive slabs of grey rock rose up into a sheer cliff, utterly impossible to climb and not coming to a stop until an escarpment 1,000–2,000 feet above. In other places the walls were less steep, and where side streams entered a line of scrub willow came down too. These woody areas made excellent camp sites because there was plenty of shelter from any evening breeze and we were able to make a generous camp fire from dead branches. We had no stove, in order to save weight, and fortunately it turned out that it was unnecessary.

The following day the number of eddies increased and though the current was still rapid by ordinary standards, the standing waves were less dangerous. It was obvious that the river was deeper and the gradient slackening off. We were nearing the sea. We stopped talking about the river and now thoughts turned to the next overland stretch—a pass through the mountains to Nørdre Strømfjord, the largest fjord in west Greenland.

A side current led us conveniently under the bank into a natural harbour and we were able to unload with ease. As we stepped out we felt like mariners going ashore on a safe new landfall.

The canoes were fixed to frames and hoisted on our backs. Soon we were trudging through the tundra flowers towards the pass. Now that the dangers of the river were over it seemed easy to carry the heavy packs. I noticed a large patch of mushrooms, enormous ones; not being absolutely certain that they were non-poisonous we ate a test amount for supper. If we became sick in the night, then they could be discarded. But they tasted fabulous and we all slept soundly. So breakfast consisted of the biggest fry-up ever.

The route consisted of short portages and long paddles through eight lakes. The wild reindeer had left a good wide track that made the distances between water trivial. In many places one would have liked to linger but though the days were hot with clear blue skies the nights were becoming noticeably colder. Each morning we found a heavy dew on our sleeping-bags. Soon that would be hoar frost and autumn would be on us. We had to press on.

One afternoon when we were poling our way through a deep

sluggish stream we noticed the remains of a Greenlander's hunting camp on the bank. Some blackened stones from their fire, piles of shrubs used for bedding and many antlers covered this grassy spot. Lying in the fireplace was the skull and beak of the great sea eagle, one of the rare birds of Greenland. It is a pity that these magnificent creatures are shot—as is every other large bird—by the Eskimoes; this is the worst aspect of their way of life. Shortly after leaving the place we saw a shadow on the water beside the kayak and looking up we saw another eagle forlornly soaring above us and warily watching our movements. This must have been the mate of the dead bird. During the whole expedition we saw only one other eagle, although there were many smaller birds of prey.

After three days we came to the last lake of the pass and now below us lay Nørdre Strømfjord—a great expanse of blue water dissected by hundreds of islands and peninsulas. As we descended I noticed with trepidation that although the weather was fine, large waves with white caps could be seen in the middle. What would the fjord be like in bad weather, I wondered? Had we taken on too much? Would the open fjord canoeing be more dangerous than the river? It seemed then a bleak prospect since our food supplies were limited. At home studying the maps in our cosy flat these inland waters had looked so sheltered. Had I made a miscalculation? However, it was evening; we were tired and hungry and this was tomorrow's problem.

As we came over the last crest before the water's edge, half a dozen tents came into view. Eskimo women and lots of children were busy stewing up the evening meal. Obviously the men were out hunting. Great haunches of reindeer and antlers were everywhere. We tried to communicate with them but it was no good—in fact, although I have travelled in many parts of the world using sign language, it was dismally unsuccessful here. Later in the evening we saw the men returning, each staggering under the weight of reindeer meat. The men were utterly exhausted and had a glazed blank look as they passed our orange tent and blue canoes. The women-folk hurried to the river to fetch water. The tent doors were shut and we had no further contact. It seemed odd that our extraordinary visit had not aroused more excitement.

In the morning we swapped a packet of cigarettes for a haunch of venison—an exchange with which they seemed delighted. Obviously meat was plentiful and smokes short. I was very impressed that they brought back all of the animal. not merely the best parts. Even the hooves were being used for jelly. On the other hand the rusty guns must have been inefficient. One was pre-1900. Many animals must be wounded and stagger off to die somewhere else.

It was a lovely morning again and there was only the faintest ripple on the fjord. My fears of last night now seemed unfounded. It was my turn to go in the single kayak—a quite different experience from sharing the double. All one's senses are keen and the day's events long remembered. I glided easily through the water below dark, steep fjord cliffs. Guillemots flashed past the bows of the canoe every few minutes, their red legs making a fine splash of warm colour. Eider ducks jostled their young families along the shore and overhead an Arctic skua was molesting a seagull. We made good progress along the coast, sometimes hugging the cliffs and sometimes heading out into the fjord to take a short cut around a headland. There was a gentle lazy swell that added just a pleasant amount of interest to the feel of the craft. Occasionally a feather floated past. Time passed quickly.

A fine bay camp site appeared, and since our next move was to cross over the seven miles or so of open fjord it was obviously better to stop now and leave that major move until the fresh energy of morning. It turned out to be an old Eskimo hunting settlement. There was a fine sea trout stream and anchorage in the corner. Unfortunately we were still too early for the Arctic char and the river contained only the small resident fish. Several stone graves containing whitened human bones showed that the spot had been used for many years. The natives had only left a day or two before, there were many half eaten dried sea trout on the ground, no doubt trapped by a net in the bay. Since the river fishing was no good, and we had no net, I went to look for blueberries on the low hill behind the camp. They were numerous and fat. I disturbed a fat ptarmigan and six fledglings intent on the same purpose; they were very reluctant to fly away.

Contrary to our expectation, the traverse of Nørde Strømfjord was not dangerous. It was a fine morning. The sea was calm and the sky blue. One could not have asked for more ideal weather to make the exposed crossing. With our foot-controlled rudders we headed straight across to an extraordinary Ailsa Craig-like promontory that was only joined to the land proper by a stone beach. We made good progress to begin with but then it seemed the crags were getting no nearer. Roger in the single was falling noticeably behind. We paddled more firmly but still the cliffs seemed reluctant to close. Soon we were paddling flat out and as we neared the rocks we realised that we were in a contrary tide race. Seen against the still rocks a very impressive current was sweeping seaward. We rounded a point and came on a cliff dotted with cormorant nests. The birds were very wary and took off immediately. They would not trust anybody in Greenland.

At a storm-beach isthmus we stopped and had lunch. It was gloriously sunny and good to have the major crossing behind us. We felt we had already had a representative sample of the fjord canoeing and it was going to be all right. As we tucked into our lifeboat biscuits and Cadbury's chocolate there was, however, one other difficulty in our minds—food. No fjord cod had bitten our spinner on the way over and the fact began to emerge that they don't venture into this glacier water of the inner fjords. One can catch them easily out at the real coast but in this silt water there is no food for them.

Brilliant sunny conditions went on day after day and so we made steady progress from camp to camp. Each evening the tent was pitched in another glorious site and a fire lit after a short search for wood. While one of us made the soup and stew from dehydrated meat, the others would collect blueberries for dessert and these were very plentiful. When this happens day after day it is difficult to imagine any change in the weather. So when one day it was cloudy and overcast we felt cheated. The rain started gently like a Scotch mist, and took some time to penetrate our clothes. But it was absolutely unrelenting and our emergency tent leaked like a sieve. Suddenly we had a brilliant idea—to balance one of the canoes upside down over the tent. The poles took the weight well and the water-tightness was made complete by hanging drapes from the side of the cockpit. Soon we had a tent which though pitch dark inside was dry. But it was just as well there was no wind; with the slightest gust the whole thing would have collapsed.

A strong sun finally dried up the rain, though for a time patches of puffy white fog stayed in the recesses of the fjord. It was just fabulous canoeing as the mist cleared to reveal a deep blue sky.

We were now canoeing towards the remarkable isthmus which separates the Nørdre Strømfjord from Arfersiorfik fjord, its neighbour in the north. This neck of land means that any boat which cannot be carried must make a detour of three hundred and fifty kilometres should it want to go north. As soon as we landed we found that our idea of portaging the crafts over the isthmus was not a new one. Red and green paint on the rocks showed that the Greenlanders had had similar ideas. I also found a rowlock in the willow scrub which, no doubt, the exasperated owner had spent many hours looking for in some time past. That night I laid out my sleeping-bag on the ground in the open while Bill and Roger decided to put up the tent, there wasn't really room for three of us to sleep comfortably in it. About 5 a.m. I felt the first rain drops on my face. The dawn was dismal and sullen, and being keen on a bit more sleep I crawled alongside the canoe and lifted it over me so that the cockpit coaming came all around. The rain bounced on the rubber skin a foot or so above my head but

I was absolutely snug. The only difficulty was that one could hardly move at all.

As we paddled out north into Arfersiorfik I felt as if a new chapter had started. We were over half way on our two hundred and fifty-mile journey to Christianshåb. All was not rosy, however, since our food supplies were running down, mainly because we were still unable to catch any fjord cod on the spinner that was trawled behind the canoe. In addition the weather was still uncertain, with sullen grey clouds taking all the life out of the scenery. We pulled into the west bank of Arfersiorfik to camp and at dinner ate a little farther into our reserves of dehydrated meat. Tomorrow we would cross the fjord and go north to Eqalugarssuit river, whose Eskimo name means "trout": surely our fishing would be more successful there? However, five miles of open fjord separated us from this river and in the morning high winds and white caps made the crossing unthinkable. The shortage of food made the waiting all the more difficult; our minds burned with the question— would the weather be all right tomorrow?

Bill felt the inactivity more than the rest of us and he was up at 4 a.m. to make sure of not missing any early morning calm. The dawn was scarcely promising. The sky was overcast and grey. Certainly there were no white horses but it looked as if a gale could appear at any minute. As we supped porridge, things seemed to improve a little, though this was probably just dawn coming. Once off there was no real turning back. I swung the rudder round into the bleak greyness beyond, paddling much firmer than normal our canoe was soon leaving the shore and safety far behind. As we approached the middle the waves grew bigger and more turbulent. I just hated every minute of the crossing since there was no real exhilaration, only the cold threat of an overturn and certain death. It was a really miserable morning to die. In the chaotic water Bill and I soon lost sight of Roger in the single canoe. We were on our own. We had to balance the canoe all the time by watching the large waves, so there was no time to look for him. Even though the breakers were within the capabilities of the craft, I knew that if the wind strengthened we might easily overturn, then rapidly perish in the icy water. I was almost more worried about the anticipation of a real gale than by the immediate dangers. But the great advantage of a canoe is its speed. We were making over four miles per hour; therefore the time of risk was short and soon we began to feel some lee from the crags ahead. When we were out of danger I had no feeling of relief; only the hollow fear that comes after taking a silly premeditated risk. And this feeling was strengthened half an hour later when, with a gale force wind, the whole fjord turned into a mass of white horses.

We climbed up the steep ground ashore and were happy to see that Roger was safely through the worst.

At the trout river we found lots of old Greenlander encampments. There were fish bones everywhere. The river stones had been reorganised to make the fish run up narrow channels. There, presumably, the Eskimoes had nets waiting for them. Obviously the fishing was excellent. I was glad that we did not have to share it with them as I fixed up a fishing-rod and selected a fat juicy Glasgow worm. I could already see the trout in the pools—they had a peculiar grey-blue colour. The only difficulty was that none of them were interested in my delectable bait. Time and time again the worms ran down past them and they took no notice. If they weren't going to play fair neither was I since we were absolutely depending on a fish supper. We declared all-out war. On the bank was an old Eskimo net fish trap—like a lobster pot—with an entrance hole at one end tapered inwards. The others were sceptical that this Heath Robinson contraption would work and grudgingly helped me move stones so that the main stream led straight into its entrance. I repaired one or two holes in the side, then wedged it in position. I knew we had two factors on our side; the full moon, which would bring an especially high tide, and the date —this last week in August is the height of the autumn spawning run. Obviously there was no point in watching the trap so I went down to the beach to collect mussels. At least they would provide a certain, if meagre, course. An hour after high water I went to see the score. Looking in the top I could see nothing in the dark water so to make sure I lifted it out—full of flapping fish. The netting was on the verge of breaking, so I rushed to the edge and dumped the fish a safe distance, then shouted to the others. The next morning we had another great bit of luck. I found a sea trout which had got itself stuck between stones— only its large tail sticking out. In a very unsportsmanlike way we tied a noose around the tail, then pulled—and the large flapping monster was ours.

With our stomachs full of trout and mussels we set off more optimistically. I was in the single, so left first as was our custom. We found the double went about 4½ m.p.h. and the single 1 m.p.h. slower, so the usual plan was for the one-man canoe to set off first whilst the others did the washing-up. First there was an open bit of coast, but since the bad weather was now replaced by fine calm weather, and a blue sky containing the faintest cirrus clouds, I enjoyed every minute. Ahead was a narrows and I wondered which way the tide would be going. Luck was with us and I was sucked through at a great rate. A fine little island appeared close to the coast; it was shaped like a turtle's back because of the smooth glacial rock. On the crest were a patch of scrub willow, cranberry plants, blueberries and moss. And scattered everywhere in the sheltered places were old eider duck nests. We lit a cosy fire and sat down to lunch on our carefully counted biscuits. After a nap in the warm afternoon sun we headed north again over some exposed choppy water to camp near the Nordenskjold glacier narrows. We had made over twenty miles. It was good to make this big mileage; it meant we had only sixty more miles to do for Christianshåb, and we were conscious that apart from the lack of food, autumn was catching us up. It was August 25th. We had our first night frost on the night of 18th/19th; already the blueberries had withered away and the leaves on the willow trees were deep red. A day ahead, we knew, we would have a high lake to cross, into which glaciers from the Inland Ice calved many bergs; would this lake be frozen? Even a few centimetres of ice would be a major obstacle to a canoe and the lake was nearly ten miles long.

After supper I went for a walk alone up the hills behind our shore camp. It is only when you walk in a country that you get any real feeling of it. I just hated having to rush on each day because of the shortage of food and time. The fact is, I felt so at home wandering in the tundra lands, I was really rather loth to arrive at Christianshåb, with all its hubbub and tele-grams. I had felt the same after crossing the ice-cap; once we had beaten the bogy of the melt-water and crevasses the journey was over, and getting down to the U.S. base and S.A.S. lounge at Søndre Strømfjord was really ghastly anti-climax. But I longed for the family—I only knew now how they were part of my life—especially since we have all been on so many expeditions together.

I scrambled up the summit crest of the hill along a well-worn fox track. Now I could see over the back and could make out all the complex fjord systems at a glance. The night frost was coming on and the waters were so calm I could almost imagine them frozen. A dull rumble reminded me of the nearness of the Nordenskjold glacier—no doubt another berg being calved. Myrtle would already have the children in the sleeping-bag at Angujartorfik. I wondered if she had made friends with the Eskimoes. Soon we would be together again.

Next morning we had the narrows to negotiate. Obviously the tides were going to be critical here since there was a vast area of sea water to flow in and out through the hundred-yard exit. We made good progress to begin with. Then we realised the tide was changing. There were two streams in opposite directions. We quickly got into the right line but in doing this we had to cross the junction, where there were large whirlpools with deep vortices. By the far side of the narrows the inward flow was petering out. However, we were now entering the great amphitheatre bay in front of the glacier, so the current was slack.

I had been looking forward to canoeing past this great glacier front ever since we left Angmagssalik. There are few finer natural wonders than the great face of a glacier teetering into the sea—it's the scale of the great sculptured face that is so impressive, and the deep blues and greens of the ice laid down possibly millions of years ago far away in the Inland Ice. Every now and then a roar and fall of ice reminded you that it is a living moving thing and that you can go close only at your peril.

The glacier is, of course, named after A. E. Nordenskjold, the great Swedish explorer—the discoverer of the North-east Passage and who also tried to cross the ice-cap from here in 1880 but was eventually forced to retrace his steps. His supply ship the *Sophia* was anchored in a bay just north of the glacier front, so we planned to camp there for the night and look for relics. It was a lovely spot with plenty of firewood, but in spite of a prolonged search there was nothing to be found. A seal bobbed up several times in the bay and a long lingering sunset made the great glacier first orange, then red, before the sun left us with a keen frost.

Next day, the 27th, we paddled up the long north-west arm of the inlet to camp at its head. This site was a veritable warren of foxes' lairs and they were very cheesed-off at being disturbed. There were three of four families, mostly black in colour, but some white—all with large sandy burrows. Most welcome was an extensive mussel bed on the beach and as the tide went out we were able to collect enormous quantities. The trouble is, of course, that they are really an *hors d'œuvre* and there was too little to follow except diluted soup and a jealously guarded biscuit. In the evening Billy made a useful recce of the hill behind, for tomorrow our route lay over an 800-foot col to our next useful piece of water, a long glacier lake.

We were now very adept at carrying the canoes assembled on the aluminium pack frames, so we made steady progress up the steep grassy slope. The weather was warmer and we were no longer worried that the glacier lake would be frozen. Nevertheless it was good to reach the summit of the glaciated slabs and rest. A flock of geese flew over, cackling furiously. They were obviously congregating for their great flight south. Some people say they fly down the edge of the ice-cap. It seems rather unfair that having brought up their broods in such a hard country they should now have to face the guns in the stubble fields and marshes at home.

From the col it was now an easy dawdle to reach the grey glacier lake. The shore was rather barren but the wall of ice behind was very fine. Rumbles and crashing ice every few minutes indicated that it was moving much faster than the Nordenskjold. While enjoying this sight there is always the danger of a particularly large ice-fall which could swamp the canoes. So having seen our fill, we now paddled briskly away towards the outlet of the lake.

Here there were hundreds of grounded bergs. It was a cheer-less place to camp and there was little wood. Billy went off to recce the river which was to take us back to the sea. Roger and and I wandered up a small stream to see if any char were around; alas, there were lots of fry but no big fish.

Next day we meandered between the bergs in the canoes, and were soon gripped in the river current. The first half mile was O.K. but beyond this the river disappeared into a thundering gorge which was utterly impossible. We descended by a series of fast canoe stretches, then by portaging across bends or gorges. The last mile or so was a deep, fast stretch which took us effortlessly all the way to the sea.

It was good to be back in salt water again, and as we went NNE along the fjord inlet we felt an increasing ocean swell. It was rather pleasant. The weather was overcast and sullen but quite calm. What worried us was the last open bit of water across to the Christianshåb peninsula. Would the weather hold to let us across tonight? We could see rain and snow flurries to the north and east and there was no time to linger. There were some magnificent castle icebergs in Disko Bay, and we could now see odd fishing-boats in the distance. For the last part we went flat out. Victory was now in sight since we could always reach the settlement on foot. The canoes surged through the water without strong paddling. Fortunately the short rations were having no effect yet. Soon the shore line was coming up —we could see the driftwood; the weather held up and this difficult crossing was over.

The tent was thankfully pitched on a bone dry promontory of moss at the head of an inlet. We could now afford to eat all our food reserves and we spent the evening sitting round our fire admiring the massive icebergs in the bay.

Overnight the cloud disappeared and a brisk on-shore breeze was sweeping in from the east by morning. This freshened during breakfast. Obviously, in the wind the canoe journey was going to be difficult, with the possibility of delay, and as our food was now almost non-existent, it was decided that Billy should walk over the hill and herald our arrival—and buy massive quantities of food to satisfy us on arrival. He went off, leaving Roger and I to paddle along the coast, taking every fragment of lee that offered. But after the shelter of Nûk Island we entered the full force of the wind coming directly on to our shore. Nor were there any islands off the coast to give a shred of shelter. I glanced quickly at Roger's canoe. The waves were so big that the front third of the craft was sometimes out of the water. Worse still, even with desperate paddling, we were only just gaining against the wind. We turned about with difficulty and hurried back into the lee of Nûk. We made lunch out of the last biscuits and soup. Now there was no meat-bar left. We fell asleep on the moss.

As often happens in these regions, the wind slackens in the evening though leaving a big sea running. The difficult stretch of water was only about one and a half miles in extent but for the whole of that part shore cliffs meant we would be unable to land. Once we really started there would be no turning back. However, strengthened by lunch and our afternoon nap, we felt ready for the challenge. We paddled the two canoes strongly out into the turbulent grey water. All the loads had been reorganised to lower the centre of gravity and I took out my seat so I was sitting on the canoe hull. In this way the chance of an overturn was minimised.

In a few minutes we were in the worst of the water. The little canoes were tossed up and down like corks. But we realised we were masters of the situation. Instead of feeling stress we were exhilarated. We paddled strongly and confidently ahead and the great sea cliffs on our right moved past quickly. The sky was quite clear and the sun was setting behind the great icebergs of Disko Bay. Now we were in the lee of the islands off Christianshåb. In the dusk we could just make out the buildings of the little settlement.

Just then we heard the chug chug chug of a diesel engine and a Trading Company boat came round from behind an island. It was coming straight for us—Billy was standing in the bows.

When we reached the harbour all the Greenlanders came out to see us paddle the last part. The word had passed quickly around the small community. It was a marvellous welcome and we felt very moved. Kye Hanson of the Greenland Trading Company gave us a splendid meal and as we lay down to sleep between the clean sheets of their guest-house we knew the journey had come to an end.

The original idea was to fly back to Søndre Strømfjod, and for me to rejoin Myrtle by the Greenland helicopter service. But this is expensive and the scheduled flights are notoriously unreliable and difficult to book. We managed to go as deck passengers on a ship down the coast but the difficulty was that no ships went up the Søndre Strømfjord, which is over a hundred miles long. Holsteinsberg was as near as we could get and the Trading Company there denied knowledge of any boats going up Søndre Strøm: later to my fury Myrtle told me that boats often go there from Angujartorfik with fresh meat. However, I knew there was an inland waterway system which almost linked with Søndre and it seemed possible we could canoe most of the distance ourselves—especially if we could get a lift for the first part. The Trading Company man immediately put us in touch with an Eskimo and soon we were chugging up

Holsteinsberg fjord in his little boat. I was jolly glad we weren't trying to do it all by canoe as there were enormous waves to begin with where the fjord was open. It began to rain; we all huddled under a tarpaulin and fell asleep.

This lift put us within twenty miles of Angujartorfik but separated by a 1,000-feet col over which we had to carry the canoes. It took two and a half days to reach the summit and from here I could look across and see Myrtle's camp about seven miles away. I would have loved to have descended then and canoed across to join her the same night; but I could see white horses caused by winds blowing up the fjord and in any case we had to go back down off the col to relay the second load up.

Descending on the Søndre Strøm side proved difficult and tedious. There was a 1,000 feet of steep polished glaciated slabs —difficult enough at the best of times but here we were stumbling under the unwieldy 17 feet 3 inch canoes on frames. I eventually found a way down a recent stone avalanche chute and was lucky enough to find a large mushroom patch. Roger and Bill had come down a much better route and were already at the fjord side. "Did you see it?" said Bill. "What?" "The musk-ox," said Bill pointing. The massive, apparently prehistoric animal was surveying our camp site critically and unenthusiastically. I quickly got out the camera and plugged in the telephoto. This seemed to annoy him intensely and he began pawing the ground. Fortunately the ground was so steep and slabby it was impossible for him to charge direct.

We all agreed that the thing to do was to go back up the hill for the second load. Surely he would then wander away. He couldn't possibly climb back up the slabs. Trying to keep out of sight we retraced our steps upwards. We had left one canoe and two heavy sacks beside a small lochan—a niche in the hillside—a 1,000 feet up. Bill and Roger made faster time up the slabs and suddenly I realised the beast was following me. I quickened my pace and the animal began to trot—it was extraordinarily nimble on the rocks. Just ahead was the crest before the lochan. I shouted to the others, who promptly launched the canoe. "Quick—jump in," they shouted as I panted to the waterside. The beast was hard on my heels. The canoe lurched sickeningly with our combined weight. There was no time to rescue the rucksack—with all our canoeing Kodachromes—which was sitting on the beach. We pushed off just as the infuriated horned monster reached the brink. We glowered at one another. I didn't know if a musk-ox could swim but we could certainly outpace him at that. Then to our horror he turned his attention to the pack and began horning it with his villanous weapons. I thought of firing a small emergency flare at him—perhaps if his coat was a little singed he would go away. Then he began tossing the sack about right on the brink. I wondered if the film tins had been done up tight. Fortunately, however, it was dusk and after half an hour of this game he trundled off into the evening gloom. We never saw him again.

Next morning we were to part. I was to canoe over the fjord to join Myrtle whilst Bill and Roger planned to stay on the north side of the fjord for the thirty-mile trip to the air base.

The others very decently waited at the camp while I did the exposed three-mile crossing. In fact, the weather was excellent and I did it in well under an hour. They also made good progress to reach the air base that night and were able to take an early plane home.

After crossing the fjord the last of my worries was gone— that is, except for the possibility of any misadventure to Myrtle and the children. I paddled lazily up the coast, then swung round into the wide Angujartorfik inlet. I could not see the tent where I left it and was a bit worried in case she had had to retreat—a child ill or something like that. As I came around the last sandbank I heard the tonk tonk tonk of an Eskimo boat coming out. As soon as they saw me they all fired their guns in welcome. Then a few more strokes and I was surrounded by them all in the camp. I could hardly tell my children from the little Eskimoes.

IX

We had a week left. Hugh had planned to spend it packing up our equipment at Søndre Strøm, but he slipped into the spell of Angujartorfik, as Heather had and I.

"*Tugtoo?*" asked Jacob, inviting Hugh to accompany him on a hunt. They set off before dawn, and I took the *umiat* out into the fjord. Hugh had said they had never caught a cod. I'd show him. "I want to come," shouted Rona, running along the beach. I put back for her, and popped her in front. We slipped out into the bay. It was empty now. The northern diver had gone and the eiders and even the ringed plovers.

I lowered my line, with three hooks attached. I immediately caught three fish. I untangled them and let them beat about the floor of our fragile little boat. "Me, me," screeched Rona, so I handed her the line.

It was marvellous that Hugh was back. I realised now how I needed him. I was incomplete without him. "Oh!" interrupted Rona. "Oh, Oh!" The water under the boat was turbulent. Something big was there. Now we really would impress Hugh. Rona and I heaved and hauled. The canoe swayed from side to side shipping water at each lurch. But I just managed to ship a paddle under the body of Rona's monster fish and heaved it aboard. Hastily we both lifted our legs over the side, as its great jaws snapped on anything available.

It was difficult to paddle in this position with my feet hanging over the side, but at last we were in shallow water, and I could wade, pulling the boat behind.

"Look at my monster," shouted Rona for all to hear. "He's enormous." I remembered the other fish and looked. They weren't there! I looked again. They definitely were not there. The still snapping jaws told me where they were and indignantly I battered the monster on the head with a paddle, then slit open his gut. Sure enough, out fell my three normal-sized fish.

179

"No one will know," I thought, as I got them ready to serve for supper. But I did not eat them myself! Hugh came back worn out, yet Jacob looked quite fresh. They carried a big stag between them, and fine fillet steak we had for supper that night, after the two pre-digested fish. Fresh, crushed blueberries for pudding, then coffee with floating fat.

We had to leave the valley a few days later. Magdalena and I clung to each other and cried. I was leaving real friends. We had come to them inquisitively and they had all looked very much the same, but we left them as individuals. As Nansen said in 1888: "One cannot help being comfortable in these people's society. Their careless ways, contentment with life as it is, and their kindness are very catching."

They had taught us far more than I could them and dif-ferences in background had melted as we got to know them. We waved and waved with both hands till the little group was swallowed up in the immensity of the Greenland scene.

I hoped fervently that my children would retain something of the gentleness and affection of their Greenland friends, who had taught them how to play for days on end without any toys. There was a tranquillity about them that I envied more and more.

Robin would now start school. Would he learn any more there of how to cope with life than he would from the Green-landers? I doubted it, as we chugged up the fjord to Søndre Strøm base.

"I'm not sure if the Copenhagen jet will land," said the airport officials. "There is a musk-ox on the runway and no one dares chase it off."

*   *   *

Soon we were soaring towards Europe. The Inland Ice slipped away below us. "See that," said an American sitting at my side. "Some damn fools crossed it on foot this year. How silly can you get?"

Copenhagen . . . T.V. cameras . . . wireless talks . . . screeches of brakes. . . . Then, at last, home. I think I will cope with the stresses and strains of civilisation better now that I know that Greenland is waiting and I can return—provided we survive the hazards of the traffic in Glasgow. The dangers of the wilds? Not nearly as bad as at home.

A letter awaited us from Carsten Berg-Sørensen of Angmagssalik. "My best bitch has had puppies, two boys and one girl. The girl is going to be good. Deep in the chest, broad in the beam and thick of thigh. I am going to call her Myrtle after you." What an honour, to think that something of me could remain in that open world in the North after all. It would be twilight now, but the fjords frozen and the dog teams straining to be off. Hansina would be snug in her kamiks and dog skin furs, and perhaps as she selected the dried tugtoo for the evening's meal, she would think of my children, or of me, and of the summer that she let us share.

APPENDIX

STRESS IN MAN: SCIENTIFIC RATIONALE OF THE EXPEDITION

by Dr. Hugh Simpson

ALTHOUGH MILLIONS OF pounds have been spent in research on the human adrenal gland and the substances it produces (steroid hormones), very little information has been forthcoming about the exact role this gland plays in protecting the organism against adverse situations. So much is this the case that in 1962 Professor Ian Bush, the well-known scientist and authority on the adrenal gland, wrote:

"Despite much work on the problem, the actions of all classes of steroid hormones at the molecular and even the cellular level remain unexplained . . . The problem remains one of the major challenges of physiology and biochemistry."

The expedition, I hoped, would result in information, hitherto unknown, of interest in this problem. Essentially the idea was to put four individuals into a very prolonged adverse situation and find out the pattern of adrenal gland activity. This pattern would give information as to how the hormones might work and at the same time make other mechanisms unlikely.

When man or animal are in an adverse situation the adrenal glands enlarge and increase the manufacture of hormones—chemicals called corticoids—which are released into the blood stream and so reach the tissues of the body. Surgical operations, written exams, burns, infections and exposure to high altitudes or cold are all situations in which this is likely to occur. While in each case there may also be some obvious local effect—such

185

as the reaction in the skin to a burn—all the situations have the adrenal gland stimulation in common, thus it is a non-specific reaction to "stress".

This discovery led to intensive research which has been channelled along two main lines of investigation; first, how are the remote adrenal glands—sitting atop the kidneys—galvanised into action in stress situations, and second, what are these hormones doing? Are they of advantage to the organism? Of course, by the argument of natural selection one can assume they are—but how? Would they be of value in preparing surgical patients for operation? The Nazis carried the argument on to its logical conclusion by giving drugs to Luftwaffe pilots, the theory being, of course, that they turned them into "supermen" who would be able to survive any stress. In fact the master-men idea was not proved by results; it seems that the normal adrenal can supply all necessary requirements in time of emergency.

But how does stress actually result in adrenal activity? It has been known for many years that the adrenals are subservient to the pituitary gland at the base of the brain. In patients, for example, whose pituitary gland is not functioning because of a tumour, or because of a clot impairing its blood supply, the adrenals shrink in size and go to "sleep". The patient becomes weak, is unable to retain salt in his body, and if untreated will die because of the dehydration which follows the salt-lack. If the patient is kept alive by consuming large quantities of salt —as was the treatment in the late 1920s before modern therapy was available—then life could be sustained for long periods; it was, however, a precarious existence and any surgical operation, infection, etc., was liable to be fatal. In other words, "stress" was lethal. It is now known that the actual link between the pituitary gland in the skull and the adrenal next to the kidney is via the blood stream; that is, the pituitary unloads adreno-trophic hormone into the veins and it then travels by the blood stream to stimulate the adrenals.

What stimulates the pituitary? This gland is about the size of a walnut and it is connected to the brain by a slender stem; of necessity all communications with the rest of the organism must pass through this and there are two possibilities. One is that stalk nerves pass down from the adjacent brain (hypothalamus) to the pituitary. However, experiments on animals in which the stalk has been cut indicate that pituitary and adrenal function are not permanently interfered with. This and other experiments seem to rule out a simple nerve connection since this would be irreparably damaged by such a procedure. However, if as with the pituitary–adrenal link, the connection was by a chemical passed in the blood stream, these experimental observations could still be explained—for vessels will heal across a wound. Thus it is currently believed that the hypothalamus manufactures a substance which passes down the stalk in special blood vessels to the pituitary, where the adrenal stimulating hormone is released. The hypothalamus itself has extensive nervous connections with other parts of the brain—both with the higher conscious centres and with other areas concerned with stress at an unconscious level. It seems, then, that it represents the exchange into which the various stress impulses arrive before being directed along the final common pathway to stimulate the adrenal. In a burn, for instance, the activation of the hypothalamic centres would occur both directly by nervous impulses from the part and indirectly through the subject's conscious fear. In pure mental stress—as occurs when students take exams—the amount of adrenal stimulation will therefore depend on the individual interpretation; thus stress could be high in the man out to get top honours as well as in the student worried about failing. In the couldn't-care-less candidate, of course, it will be zero.

At the peripheral end of this stress pathway we have the release of corticoids. What do these substances do? How do they ameliorate the effects of stress? No one knows the precise answer to these questions and the best that one can do is to consider possibilities. A trivial injury (e.g. a thorn prick)—not followed by a non-specific adrenal stress response—has a simple and effective healing process to restore normality. But if the injury were massive the life of the organism could be threatened and then it might be of survival advantage to restrain normal healing processes, otherwise they might of themselves demand too much of the available resources. By exercising such restraint the adrenal hormones could give benefit in this way. Certainly an important action of these substances is to damp down the so-called inflammatory reaction seen externally as swelling and redness, and also healing.

Another interesting property of the adrenal hormones is that they inhibit division of body cells necessary to maintain the status quo in many of our tissues. Skin, for example, is being shed all the time and needs to be constantly replaced (a fact that the drandruff advertisements cash in on) and this is effected by a multiplication of cells in the deeper layers. In stress this maintenance is slowed. Two temporary advantages could come from this; one is that the raw materials may be redirected for more vital work, and second, a cell in the process of division (mitosis) is temporarily unable to carry out any specialised function (e.g. a gland is unable to produce hormones). It is interesting that tissues which have to maintain themselves by cell division usually wait until the night to do this, when stress is least likely.

But many stresses are not simple injuries and may be purely mental worry (e.g. sitting examinations). Of what possible advantage could the stress response be then? The answer is, none that we know of. In primitive life mental stress was usually followed by physical combat and injury, and it might be that this reaction is an evolutionary hangover. The anti-inflammatory and anti-mitotic actions of these substances is undoubted but the interpretation of these effects as a "stalling" of the metabolism in severe stress is speculative. Possibly in the next ten years or so more research will clarify the rationale of these inhibitory effects. But do the adrenal hormones do anything positive? Do they promote adaptation to stress or are these merely local phenomena in the tissues? Do they promote the manufacture of new intracellular enzymes—in particular stressed tissues—necessary to gear the tissue to greater turnover? At present the evidence is sketchy. In a prolonged major mental and physical stress is there, in fact, any adaptation at all?

The object of our Greenland Expedition was to study the pattern of adrenal gland response in a very prolonged stress situation, i.e. ski-ing four hundred miles over an uninhabited ice desert with all the stress of physical endurance, threat of starvation, anticipation of crevasses and so on. Since the stresses would be more or less constant from day to day in this featureless country with no radio contact, then any results obtained should be easy to interpret. Three outcomes seemed possible: first, the adrenal response might be steady for the whole of the month-long trip; second, there might be a progressive increase in adrenal output because of a mounting need for stress hormones; and third, an initial brisk response might fall to zero even though the stress was sustained, indicating adaptation.

Such an experiment is, of course, almost unique, as there are so few other human stress situations which can be studied for so long; experimental subjects are hard to come by!

Apart from obtaining interesting facts about the effects of prolonged stress, I thought insight would be obtained into the so-called stress diseases. These are again a controversial subject but there is apparent clinical correlation between day-to-day human stress situations and peptic ulcers, coronary thrombosis, high blood pressure, etc. The worried man develops an ulcer. But are these diseases *caused* by the increased adrenal activity or not? We have only the hard facts that worry causes ulcers and it also causes increased adrenal activity. In our Greenland experiment a continuous stress response throughout the crossing would support the idea of stress diseases, whereas an adaptive response would not, i.e. confirming that the man in a job beyond his capacity is in a state of permanent adrenal excess.

In the experiment I planned to estimate adrenal activity by collecting urine samples and bringing these back to Glasgow for the difficult analysis of corticoid hormones. It is fortunate that the urine outputs of these substances give a good indication of the gland's activity and are a good deal less painful to obtain than blood specimens! Moreover, the Glasgow University department where I work under Professor Symington specialises in these estimates, which have only recently become practicable.

Normal hormone levels were established while the party waited at Angmagssalik. With all our preparations for the crossing completed, we relaxed on the East Greenland coast for a week in comfort and diverted by the social round. The mean of the values obtained for each subject during this period has been called 100 per cent. In Myrtle a figure of 9·2 mg. per day was obtained. For the three males (Roger, Hugh and Bill) the figures were 17·2, 10·7, and 15·0 mg.

In three of the subjects the authentic (non-stress) nature of these control values was confirmed by comparison with previous readings during a Scandinavian holiday.

During the first five days of the ice-cap journey, when we sledged over hazardous sea-ice then up a steep glacier, there was a dramatic rise of output in the 17-hydroxycorticosteroids (pooled mean = 161 per cent) and these high levels were sustained over the next five days when we were still climbing towards the 8,150-foot ice-cap summit (pooled mean = 167 per cent). During the subsequent fifteen days the party travelled fast over easy, level surfaces, and the five-day means fell successively (158, 141 and 133 per cent). Stress during this stage was largely physical—250 miles were covered in 12 days.

Then followed three five-day periods during which we descended from the ice-cap, and the hormone levels rose again to 154, 151 and 158 per cent. These increases corresponded closely to the increased stress experienced in traversing the thaw zone where rivers, morasses, crevasses and finally giant ice hummocks made progress desperately slow. After we had reached the security of the U.S. base at Søndre Strømfjord, lower but still above normal levels were observed over the week of measurement, the mean value being 128 per cent.

What light do these results throw upon the role of adrenal

hormones in the response to stress? Is it that they are only necessary at the initial impact of the stress, and that having effected a change in peripheral cells they are no longer needed? Might they, for example, be concerned with the formation of new intracellular protein? This is one concept of adaptation. Alternatively, they might be essential for the sustenance of stressed cells throughout the adverse period.

Our results demonstrate that no adaptation took place, since throughout the journey changes in steroid excretion paralleled the changing degrees of stress encountered.

Hugh and Roger, the joint leaders, recorded their highest levels during the first five-day period when they were faced with making a critical decision, which could have proved disastrous, concerning the route to be taken to the ice-cap. Bill's highest readings were recorded after he had made a navigational error resulting in a detour. Myrtle's readings remained high after the period of major stress, a finding which correlates with the fact that she was extremely exhausted by the final effort of reaching safety.

On attempting to obtain a second set of control readings in the U.K., unexpectedly high levels were obtained—in some instances as high as those obtained on the ice-cap. Twelve observations were made on random days while subjects were at their normal occupations. Myrtle is an author and housewife, Bill a company secretary, myself, a University lecturer, and Roger a school-teacher. These are responsible and, to a certain extent, competitive jobs, and it is apparent that such occupations may involve far more stress and adrenal cortical stimulation than has been recognised. These figures contrast with those obtained from the same subjects during rest periods. They accord with the fact that people in Western civilisations tend to have high steroid outputs, and with my own observations (*J. Endocr.*, 1965, 32, p. 179) that food gathering Amerindians in the Surinam jungle have much lower corticoid outputs than medical students in Glasgow.